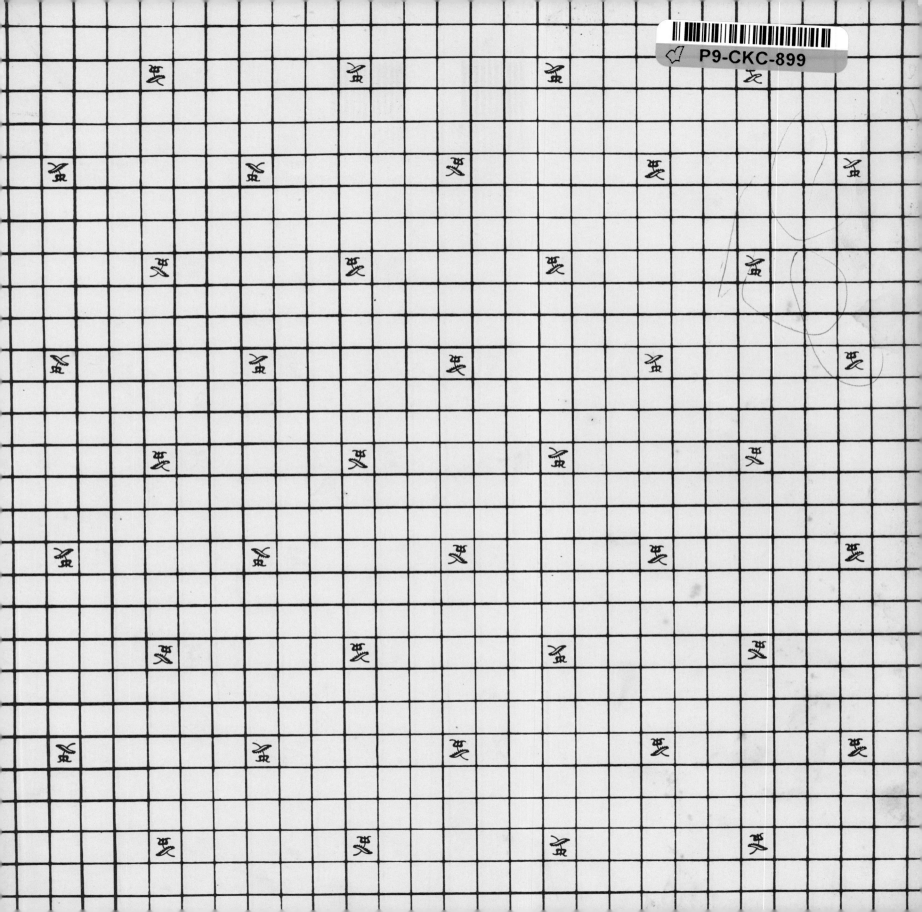

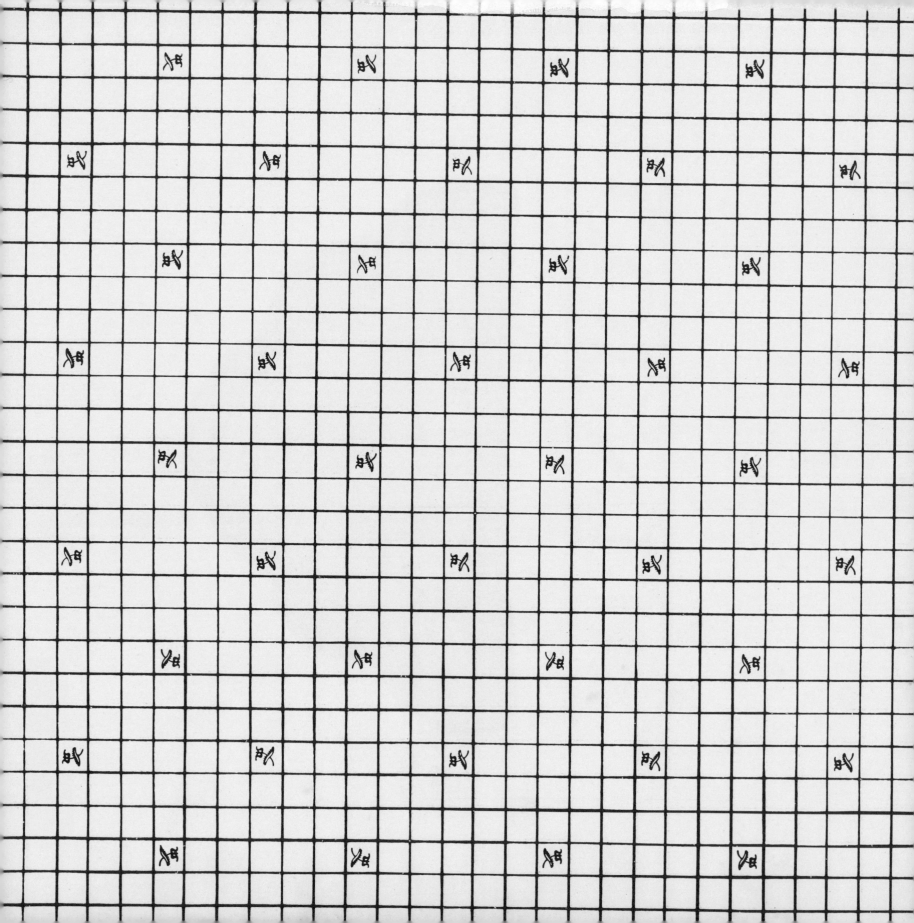

AMERICAN
COUNTRY

AMERICAN
COUNTRY
A STYLE AND SOURCE BOOK

BY MARY ELLISOR EMMERLING

DESIGN BY RAYMOND WAITES

FOREWORD BY DR. ROBERT BISHOP, DIRECTOR, MUSEUM OF AMERICAN FOLK ART

TEXT BY ELIZABETH WARREN
DESIGN ASSOCIATE: JANICE WARNER
RESEARCH ASSOCIATE: BARBARA KRAVETZ

Clarkson N. Potter, Inc./Publishers NEW YORK
DISTRIBUTED BY CROWN PUBLISHERS, INC.

TO
MY DAUGHTER,
SAMANTHA, AND SON,
JONATHAN

Clarkson N. Potter, Inc.
A division of Crown Publishers, Inc.
One Park Avenue
New York, New York 10016

Published simultaneously in Canada by
General Publishing Company Limited.
Printed in Japan

Library of Congress Cataloging in
Publication Data
Emmerling, Mary Ellisor.
American country, a style and source
book.
Includes index.
1. Decoration and ornament, Rustic—
United States.
2. Folk art—United States. 3. Interior
decoration—
United States. I. Kravetz, Barbara. II.
Warren,
Elizabeth, 1950- III. Title.
NK2002.E46 1980   747'.213
79-23666
ISBN: 0-517-538466

15 14 13 12 11 10 9 8

Portions of this book first
appeared in *House Beautiful*.

Photo Credits: p. I, courtesy Frank Kolleogy; pp. 4–5, 14–15, 50–51, 146–147, 180–181, 208–209, courtesy
Chris Mead; pp. 40, 69, 81, 101, 137, 172, 187, 189, 191, courtesy *House and Garden*, Copyright © 1978 by
The Condé Nast Publications Inc.; pp. 111, 112, 159, 160, 172, 179, courtesy *Mademoiselle*, Copyright © 1976
by The Condé Nast Publications Inc.; pp. 41, 58, 68, 69, 155, 161, 172, 186, reprinted by permission of
House Beautiful, © 1979, The Hearst Corporation, all rights reserved.

ACKNOWLEDGMENTS

This book has come to life from years of collecting and loving American country furniture and antique accessories. It is from all those flea markets, antiques shows, and shops—especially from Joel and Kate Kopp's "America Hurrah," where my collecting began thirteen years ago. It has grown from those little special things that found a place in my home and became collections years later—like my hearts and watermelons.

One of the most wonderful things about bringing this book together has been the people I have met. They are the ones who have made *American Country* so special to me and now, I hope, to you too:

to all the people who let us come into their homes and lives and photograph their American antiques—it is their taste in living with American antiques that we wanted to show here;

to the photographers credited on each page, whose time and caring went into this book—and without whom it would never exist; special thanks to Chris Mead, J. Barry O'Rourke, and Frank Kolleogy who never complained about the long hours and weekends, and who worked on the book with a love I will never forget; to the photographers who let us use the photographs from their files, especially Robert Perron, Karen Radkai, and Otto Fenn; to *House Beautiful* and *House & Garden* for permission to use their copyrighted photographs; to Joe Ruggiero and everyone at Ethan Allen who works on the wonderful slide shows shown in their galleries throughout America for their photographs; to the numerous manufacturers credited throughout for lending photographs of their products for the Directories; and to all the antiques dealers who sent back responses for the Antiques Directory;

to all the directors and staffs of the museums we photographed for their time and kindness, with special thanks to John Rice Irwin at the Museum of Appalachia, where I was moved to tears by the years and effort that his family has devoted to this spectacular private museum and who fed us some wonderful home-cooked meals with ingredients from their garden;

to the many dealers who patiently answered our questions and gave us their secret sources; my special thanks to Helaine Fendelman, who pulled out all her sources and opened doors for us all over the country; to Barbara Pollack in Illinois, who also opened new cities, people, and states for resources we just would not have found; to Robert Kinnaman and Brian Ramaekers in Texas, who became friends immediately and introduced us to Beverly and Tommy Jacomini, who not only opened their doors but gave us a wonderful farm to photograph; to Beverly who made us go back to Houston to have a country-western dinner at the Hofbrau; to Edwa Osborn who is a sweetheart and believes in the heart; to Rod Kiracofe and Michael Kile who helped us in California;

to a longtime friend and dealer, Gayle Young, whose "welcome friends" rug opens this book;

to everyone at Mädderlake florist, who were there when we needed flowers in ten minutes, with special thanks to William Jarecki, Tom Pritchard, Pat Braun, and Alan Boehmer;

to Clare Hamm, who typed my first proposal;

to Barbara Kravetz, who made this book possible, for all the research, organization, and phone calls, and for never getting hassled or hurried—she kept us together when we thought we couldn't go on, and I will never forget it;

to Liz Warren, whose writing, interviews, and research gave special depth to the information in this book;

to Gayle Benderoff, my agent, who made the phone call that started this book and made my dreams come true;

to Russ Berman who read my contracts;

to my mother, father, brothers, Terry and Steve, and sister, Nancy, who have always been there when I needed them; to John, who for ten years allowed me to do my country look and gave me the space to do it in; to Juanita Jones, who took care of Jonathan and Samantha while I worked on this book; to Susan MacWhinnie, Susan Sawrey, and Ann Emmerling who were there when Juanita needed a break;

to everyone at *House Beautiful,* especially JoAnn Barwick and Norma Skurka, who let me do this book and keep my job and were very supportive; to Joan Pascale, who kept it all running while I was running; to Jason Kontos and Barbara Brooks for being there when I couldn't be;

to Raymond Waites, the designer of *American Country,* who made me realize that fate is what it is all about—we met at the right time to make this the best dream possible—and to Susan Lewin at *House Beautiful* who couldn't do a shooting with Raymond and asked me to fill in; to Janice Warner at Gear Design who did it all—the layouts were superb and although the hours were long and tedious, she never complained; to everyone at Gear who helped along the way;

to my friends at *Mademoiselle* magazine, my home for the last twelve years, where I learned everything—especially to Edith R. Locke and to Dona Guimaraes, the best teacher I will ever have—I will always remember to polish the apples for her; to Alexander Liberman at Condé Nast for his taste—just being around him I learned something special every day;

to all the people who have written and supported me through my years at *Mademoiselle* and *House Beautiful,* and who made me realize there was a country look I was showing that they wanted to see—all of their letters have been very special to me;

to all my friends who shared their recipes for this book, especially to Martha Stewart who introduced me to country food through her recipes, with special appreciation for her chocolate chip cookies;

to the photographers' assistants Basil Nasto and Randy O'Rourke; to Pentax for lending me a camera to catch those special moments; to Dr. Robert Bishop and all the staff at the Museum of American Folk Art in New York City, who are doing an outstanding job promoting my favorite subject;

to Duane Michals, one of my biggest supporters;

to Suzanne Slesin and Joan Kron who helped me with all the hints that got them through *High-Tech*—I am very glad to be following their book;

to the Jimmy Carter family of Virginia, whose house, as presented in *House & Garden* years ago, drew me to the country look, and special thanks to Mary Randolph Carter Berg, whose friendship at *Mademoiselle* was very special;

to Jane West, our publisher, whose great ideas made this book better, and whose suggestion to go west made the difference in reporting the country look; to my editor, Nancy Novogrod, whose support and constructive comments helped us along the way; to Michael Fragnito, who kept us on schedule, and to Pam Pollack, Ellen Gilbert, Beth Ferranti, and everyone at Clarkson Potter for keeping this book on time;

and to you, a special friend, for the support and encouragement through the long hours, days, and weeks when I thought it was all too much, who helped me find that you can do it all with a special push.

VI

CONTENTS

CHRIS MEAD

The earliest colonists in America were primarily concerned with the pursuit of religious and personal freedom and rarely attempted to cast aside family and social traditions. From the very beginning they sought to re-create in the New World the homes, the furnishings, and the life-styles that they had left behind. The now popular, romanticized concept that all 17th-century houses were fitted with modest country pieces is simply not accurate, for settlers in the major eastern seaboard cities such as Boston, New York, and slightly later, Philadelphia furnished their houses in a manner that closely approximated the richly carved and decorated medieval styles used in European homes of the same social stratum.

A curious pattern emerged. A fashion appeared at court in England when the rulers commissioned the most gifted craftsmen they could afford to create furniture for them. A style, once established by the rulers and popularized by the members at court, was then adopted by the upper classes in London, and in time it filtered down to the lower classes. Its concepts were soon transported to America's seaboard cities by the wealthy, who, in an effort to demonstrate economic superiority in their communities, imported furniture in great volume. In 1682 Mr. Fitzhugh of the Virginia Company wrote to London requesting a "feather bed & furniture, curtains & vallens. The furniture, Curtains & Vallens, I would have new, but the bed at second hand, because I am informed new ones are full of dust."

Throughout the 18th century most colonials continued to look to the Old World in matters of taste and fashion. Once a style was firmly established in a major American city, it was quickly adopted by all the craftsmen working in that city and by those in other major cities as well, for there was an extensive intercity relationship based upon commerce that depended upon the sea for its transport. New styles ultimately filtered down to the country craftsmen who, many times wisely, did not attempt to copy them exactly but relied upon free adaptations of general outline and contour, which they embellished with their own sense of design.

As the population expanded through a continual flow of new settlers and the growth of the already existing families, new settlements sprung forth at an astonishing rate. Large numbers of immigrants from various economic classes lacked the funds as well as the inclination to concern themselves with stylish furniture. Their homes, modest in size, were for the most part jammed full of utilitarian pieces, many of which were dual purpose—tables that converted into chairs, settles that became beds. The furniture crafted by people living in these new settlements away from seaboard communities were the prototypes of the true country style.

The English in New England, the Dutch in the Hudson River Valley, and other immigrant groups used the same woods for their furniture in the New World as they had in the Old. Oak, especially prized for its strength and durability, was most popular, for it could be handsomely carved and turned. By the opening of the 18th century native woods such as maple, pine, and cherry replaced oak as the favored materials. To a great extent this came about because these woods were easier to work than oak, and the finished product was not as susceptible to splintering, nor was it as brittle. Today cherry furniture is highly prized. At the time of its original use, however, cherry was considered a poor substitute for imported mahogany and inevitably was stained to look like the more expensive foreign wood. Curly maple, immensely popular with the collector today, also was considered inferior and oftentimes it was painted. A banister-back "great chair" from the Hudson River Valley, now in the collections of Greenfield Village and Henry Ford Museum, Dearborn, Mich., retains the original black paint which covers a dazzling curled maple that, through two centuries of constant wear, has become exposed.

In the 18th century several regional areas produced a truly great country style. The Germans in Pennsylvania brought with them a strong cultural heritage that extended to the decorative and visual arts. Painted and decorated furniture in the form of cupboards, tables, chairs, and especially chests attests to the pervasiveness of the inherited European tradition that found new vitality in America where in rural farming communities it inspired a brilliant, colorful, new flowering of design.

The Swedes in the Delaware River Valley crafted furniture that was distinctly their own. Unique to their communities are the mammoth armchairs with slat-backs and vigorous, bulbous-turned ball feet on the front legs and dramatic vase-and-ring-turned front stretchers. Much of their case-work was painted and decorated as well.

Without question, the heyday of the country style was the 19th century. As the opening of the second quarter dawned, improved transportation and communication were made possible by the Industrial Revolution. American life-styles changed dramatically. Machine technology provided the impetus for a true city style, where handcraftsmanship played an ever-decreasing role.

By the 1830s massive, flat-surfaced, unadorned pillar-and-scroll furniture, made of pine bodies veneered with mahogany and rosewood, became the style of the day. Country carpenters borrowed this style and further simplified it. Their rather plain pieces were then brilliantly painted and grained in attempts to simulate the imported mahogany that was the rage in the cities. The true American country style was born. It did not flourish long, however, for the availability of mass-produced, inexpensive, machine-made furniture from mail-order houses increased dramatically during the 1860s and reduced the demand for handmade objects.

During the Victorian period (the English Queen Victoria reigned from 1837 to 1901), an astonishing number of styles were popularized by American furniture manufacturers. No sooner was a fashion firmly entrenched than a new style was promoted by effective sales forces representing the furniture manufacturers. The battle of the styles in the cities many times caused confusion in rural furniture-making shops, for craftsmen would attempt to combine the best of several styles with oftentimes amusing results.

Americans celebrated the one hundredth birthday of their country at Philadelphia, where the Philadelphia Centennial was mounted in 1876. An international exposition that attempted to acknowledge America's contribution to the decorative arts through special exhibitions, the centennial spawned a new cult of people dedicated to collecting and preserving treasures from America's past. The late 19th- and early 20th-century collectors rarely looked at what we today call country furniture with anything but disdain. Their primary focus was on the 17th century and they concerned themselves with the greatest pieces of formal furniture that were still plentiful. The simple but sturdy plain styles that we today marvel at and place upon platforms and pedestals in museums and give prize positions to in our homes had to wait their turn to be appreciated.

A handful of collectors during the 1920s, 1930s, 1940s, and 1950s began to recognize that the more modest types that had originated in the country did indeed have merit. Although some of them were well made and had a sense of design, timelessness, and inherent beauty, it would be naïve to believe that all country furniture is beautiful. It is not. Just as everything that is old is not beautiful. Much was poorly constructed originally and today is still of little merit.

Collecting should be based upon the preservation of significance. Many have recognized this and beautiful, well-made decorative country pieces in the last few years have begun to command staggering prices at antiques shops, in antiques shows, and more recently at auctions. As in all collecting fields, one must be selective. Choose the best and you will have an object that is pleasing to live with and one that will appreciate in value dramatically through the years to come. Do not settle for less, for it is better to acquire one major piece than numerous modest examples of dubious value.

Fine country furniture has become so valuable that the construction of imitations is extremely profitable. An army of fakers with paintbrush in hand have skillfully learned the techniques of reproducing early painted and decorative surfaces. Beware! If you are interested in forming a collection, focus upon authentic pieces of high quality, for they alone provide the true joy of collecting.

DR. ROBERT BISHOP
Director
Museum of American Folk Art

Houses decorated with painted furniture, quilts, and baskets, tables set with stoneware and pewter, homemade breads and jellies, homegrown vegetables, traditional holiday foods and celebrations—we call this style of decorating, and of living, American Country.

While based on the past, it is a style ideally suited to active, informal life-styles of today for there are no rules to follow when assembling this highly personal look, and little upkeep is required to maintain it. It is not a style that requires a decorator to put together, although decorators of such eminence as Sister Parrish have used country furniture and accessories to create dazzling effects. All the components—quilts, baskets, plain and painted wood furniture, pottery, folk art—are available at antiques shops and shows, or through contemporary craftsmen and manufacturers who produce new objects with an old-fashioned country mood. Today, everything from furniture to fabrics, tableware, and accessories is being manufactured with the rustic look and feel of the past.

The collecting of country antiques and folk art is not a recent phenomenon. Numerous articles in *Antiques* magazine from the 1920s and 1930s dealt with "country things." But, in general, these unsophisticated objects did not benefit from the boom in formal American and European antiques during the mid-

dle years of this century. In the past decade, however, the growth in this field has been enormous, as is evidenced by such comprehensive shows as the Whitney Museum's "Flowering of American Folk Art" in 1974, and the auction of the Stewart Gregory collection at Sotheby Parke Bernet in 1979, which set new price levels for folk art.

Antique country furniture was made by hand away from urban centers. Sturdy, simple in style, and often ingenious in its solutions to design problems, many pieces varied little from one decade to the next, for they were made for customers who were more interested in durability than in the latest city styles. Frequently, country furniture reflects design features of highly styled pieces—Queen Anne, Chippendale, Hepplewhite—but the objects have obviously been re-created from memory, copied from a piece glimpsed on a visit to the city, rather than from a formal pattern book. The furniture that results, therefore, is often unique and all the more appealing for its individuality.

Much country furniture was painted, both to hide the fact that less costly woods were used and, often, that many kinds of wood were used in one piece. It was also painted for the sheer beauty of the decoration.

Most of the pieces available today were made in the 18th and 19th centuries, when

1

expansion into rural areas was at its height. This includes furniture made in all the southern and western areas where the pioneers settled, for, just as the early colonists on the East Coast were limited in the amount of furniture they could bring from Europe, so, too, did the American pioneers have to make most of their own furnishings on the frontier.

Some of the houses and apartments in this book are furnished almost entirely with these authentic objects from the past. Whether a New England farmhouse or a New Mexico adobe hacienda, these are environments with a true period look, but spaces that, because of the inherent lack of formality in the furniture and accessories, create a casual atmosphere.

Most of the interiors depicted here, however, are furnished with a combination of antiques, reproductions, and contemporary pieces, including the latest in modern industrial design. These rooms clearly show that not only do country furnishings look good in contemporary settings—the stark backgrounds offsetting the rustic shapes and colors—but the tones and textures of the old and old-feeling furnishings add the warmth that many find lacking in modern interiors.

Throughout this volume photographs of a 200-year-old barn, converted into living space as part of a "design experiment," prove how successfully old-fashioned country elements blend with the best of contemporary American design. Against a background of the old wood and stone of the barn, antique stoneware crocks, decoys, quilts, rag rugs, and, for dramatic effect, barn siding hung like artwork, blend with clean-lined multipurpose furniture, inexpensive industrial spot lighting, and up-to-date appliances. Fabrics are reminiscent of the past, many with the look of homespun textiles, but the patterns are neater, less fussy and flowery. The colors are taken from the country itself—from pumpkins, Indian corn, wood, stone. It is a look that is supremely adaptable: furnishings open for storage, rearrangement, travel from one room to another. It is a style that is an important trend in American decorating.

Some of the houses in this book are true antiques, dating as far back as the 17th century. Others are high-rise apartments, 20th-century suburban houses, or modern architectural structures. All have in common the air of informality and warmth that simple wood furniture and unpretentious accessories provide. For country is a style that, as many homeowners mentioned, is easy to maintain and perfect for families with children and pets. Scratches and dents on the furniture simply add to the character of the already well-worn pieces.

American Country is more than furnishings, however. It is also the plants you grow, the foods you cook, the decorations you use for holidays. This book includes, therefore, tips on cultivating and displaying flowers, vegetables, and herbs, favorite recipes contributed by friends and homeowners, and suggestions for making Christmas extra special, with simple, old-fashioned decorations.

Living space *in the barn is divided into four levels. The first level, the basement, houses the kitchen. The Great Hall and master bedroom and bathroom occupy the second level. The third level, an unheated transition space, is used for sleeping quarters during the summer months. Level four, the crow's nest, contains the sleeping loft seen on page 96.*

2

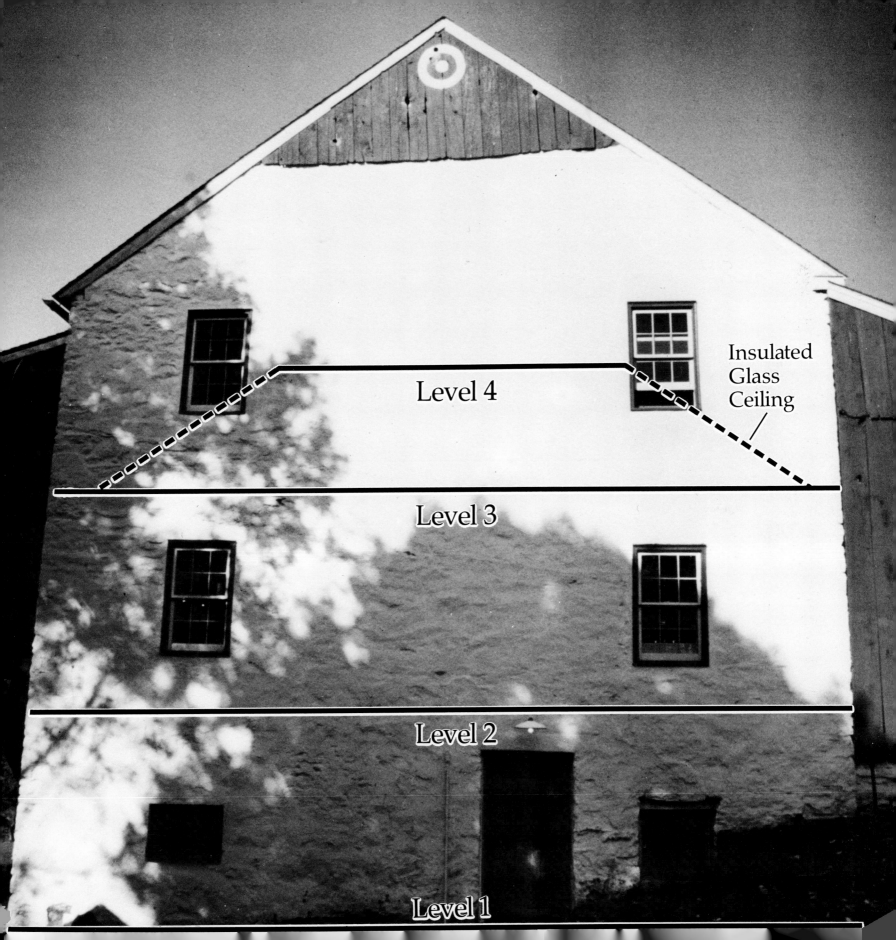

Insulated
Glass
Ceiling

Level 4

Level 3

Level 2

Level 1

As a decorating style, American Country is a look that can be put together relatively inexpensively. While the best country antiques are costly today, you can still find good pieces at reasonable prices at flea markets and country auctions. Antiques shows and shops may charge a little more, but the quality and, frequently, the guarantee of authenticity the dealer will provide may be well worth the money. The directory of dealers in the back of this book lists sources of antique country furnishings located throughout the nation.

But antiques are not necessary to create a country mood. Many firms make reproductions that are practical alternatives to more costly and rare antiques, and much of the work of contemporary craftsmen and manufacturers provides an old-time country feeling. The directory of contemporary sources provides a selective list of readily available new merchandise that blends well with country antiques and has a country feeling all its own.

Woodburning stoves, *made by Russo, heat the "great hall" of the converted barn shown on these pages. Chosen for their good design and their energy efficiency, one stove is used on each side to warm the large space. The 200-year-old barn is owned by William C. Musham and his wife, Bettye Martin.*

"Great hall," *the main living area of the barn (far left), and the rest of the first and second levels are enclosed by a Thermopane structure (below) designed to save energy by closing off the top floors in winter, while preserving the original exterior lines of the building. The barn, located on an 80-acre farm in Bucks County, Pa., was* *designed by the Gear team, headed by Raymond Waites, and built by contractor Rube Weaver. Waites used the space as a design laboratory, creating all the furniture and the fabrics (now part of the New Country Gear® collections) to express the simple country look, streamlined for today.*

7

8

Fabrics *from the New Country Gear collection for Cohama/Riverdale include "Country Basket" (top left and right), "Picnic Basket" (lower left), and "Country Daisy" (lower right). Colors for these fabrics—"Barn Rose," "Pumpkin," and "Rust" shown here—were all derived from natural objects. Fabrics are made of 100 percent cotton.*

Third level *of the barn (left) is a multifunction space, used as a den or for sleeping. The master bedroom below is seen through the Thermopane skylight.*

Platform couch *in this unheated part of the barn was purposely made the right width to allow sleeping in the warmer months. The floors are made of wood taken from old buildings in the area. Pennsylvania rag rug is antique, woven in colors that blend perfectly with the "Rust" and "Barn Rose" tones of the newly designed fabrics. Industrial-style work lamps hang from the stone wall.*

9

CHRIS MEAD

CHRIS MEAD

Contemporary bathroom, *an intended contrast to the more rustic great hall, combines modern convenience with country accessories—decoys, Shaker-style boxes, a rag rug. The beams overhead are the single reminder of the barn's past, for even the rough-hewn siding was painted white to maximize the light in the room. Countertops, platforms, and the nonskid flooring are white American Olean tile. The large white tub (the wooden steps are for climbing into it) and the sink are by Kohler. This bathroom and the master bedroom (right) are one room, combined to increase the feeling of space. From the bedroom on the second level there is a clear view through the overhead glass to the fourth level sleeping loft.*

Platform bed, *made of wood painted white, provides storage space at each end. Sheets on the bed, in "Rust" and "Wood" colors, are from the "Country Furrows" collection for Springs Mills. The rust-painted cupboard is antique.*

11

Sliding doors *separate the toilet area from the master bath beyond.*

Medicine cabinet *actually covers a window that opens onto the porch. All lighting fixtures are industrial-style lamps. Laboratory faucet is by Chicago.*

Beamed kitchen, *planned for cooking, dining, and entertaining, occupies the first level of the barn. Work space, arranged around the center island, is sufficient for guests to join in the food preparation. In the near future, when crops are again grown on this farm, canning and preserving will also take place here. All the appliances, including Amana refrigerator/freezer and Caloric cooktops and ovens, were chosen for their energy efficiency. Peg racks, reminiscent of those in Shaker dwellings, line all the walls. Tile by American Olean covers the floor and center island.*

Kitchen table *is actually two new tables, made from old wood, placed together. Old beams were used for the legs; the tops were sanded smooth. One end, fitted with old iron cow feeders, is used as a buffet server.*

Galvanized pipes, *attached to the beams, are used to hang pots and pans and utensils above the center island. Industrial-style lighting is plugged into tracks placed between the beams. Farm light below is by Abolite.*

12

I

P   A   R   T   I

COUNTRY PLACES

17

Traditionally, Americans have distinguished between country and city homes, furnishings, and even life-styles. Today, when the appeal of the country has reached out and enveloped those who were born and bred in urban centers, that distinction is blurred. Some people have given themselves completely to the country, moving to rural areas and adapting their lives to the country pace. Others escape their city life for a country house on weekends. But for many of us, the return to America's rustic roots is symbolic only, accomplished by surrounding ourselves with country furnishings. The country places presented here, therefore, are rural farmhouses and city apartments, backwoods cabins and urban row houses.

COUNTRY
IN THE COUNTRY

As this nation has grown, the location of the "country" has changed too. Once the country lay just outside the city limits. Today, most urban dwellers have to travel a good distance to find truly rural areas. But for many, the pleasures they find there are worth the trip.

All the houses in this chapter are physically located in the country. Some are used as weekend and vacation retreats, an escape from urban apartments and lifestyles, providing an opportunity to work in the garden or wander down a quiet path. Other homeowners have adopted the country life permanently, setting down roots, raising plants, livestock, and families.

Windmill, *built on Nantucket in 1746, once provided the energy needed to grind corn.*

Renovated barn *is an old structure recently converted into living space. The ground floor is now the kitchen; main living areas are on the second level.*

19

Most of the houses are old structures, rescued from decay by caring hands. Some once saw life as commercial buildings—a forge, a tavern, a general store—but as the need for these enterprises diminished, and as the demand for country housing increased, they were converted into highly original residences. Inside, whether furnished authentically to their period and location or with a combination of old and new, they reflect life in the country.

CHRIS MEAD

PARADISE ISLAND

The houses on Nantucket Island are said to have been "built with whale oil," an allusion to the island's prosperous years as a whaling port. There are approximately 400 houses here that are at least 150 years old, most furnished with the work of past and present local craftsmen. While the first houses were simple lean-tos, later structures were generally two stories, with a "three-bay" (two windows and a door) front.

Building styles *generally followed those on the mainland, but with a time lag of about 10 years.*

Shingle houses *(as shown here) and clapboard houses are most common on Nantucket Island. Shingle houses are usually left unpainted; clapboard houses are often painted white.*

21

22

TIDEWATER COLONIAL

"This is a simple, funny old house with a lot of simple, funny old furniture," says Pat Carter of her family's restored 17th-century Virginia home. "Sometimes I shudder at the way we treat some of the really good pieces we own, but this is a house that believes in living with a sense of the past, not in setting it aside."

Gateleg table *in the dining room is 17th-century English. White chairs in the background are also from England.*

Vine wreath, *made by one of the children, is decorated with fresh vegetables of the season.*

23

24

A FAMILY RETREAT

The Rappahannock River-front home of Mr. and Mrs. James Northam Carter is a wonderful complex of buildings, consisting of the restored 17th-century main house, a guest quarter, a log cabin, barn, and other outbuildings, or dependencies, as Virginians call them. "With nine children, three of us married with children of our own, this place has grown as we've grown," remarks one married daughter. "The main house is where we gather to eat, drink, dance, have a good time together. The dependencies offer us independence and privacy—individual spaces in a rare communal environment." Most of the furnishings are 18th century or older and a blend of American and European antiques. "We buy what we like, what we have a feeling about," notes Pat Carter.

Log cabin *is furnished with an antique European armoire and a primitive wood table from Virginia.*

CHRIS MEAD

The barn *is a reproduction of an 18th-century structure in Williamsburg, Va. The hayloft is dry and dark, a perfect place for drying herbs.*

TOP QUALITY

Years of buying, selling, culling, and trading up to the very best in Americana have resulted in the magnificent collection displayed in this midwestern antiques dealer's house.

Rather than re-create a period environment for his collection, the owner planned a neutral-toned, modern addition to his shop, an authentic old general store. For him, the stark whiteness of the new wing affords the best possible way to appreciate the color and form of the antiques, almost all in their original condition. And the space around each piece makes it stand out as sculpture—for these are not functional, everyday objects but museum-quality antiques to be viewed as art.

Sky-lit hallway *is lined with masterpieces of Early American craftsmanship: a very early blue-painted chest, a small New England blanket chest, Pennsylvania black toleware, painted ladder-back daybed, and a Connecticut highboy. Above, a child's toy, c. 1800.*

26

Windsor-style settee, *an unusual, sculptural shape, is from Pennsylvania, c. 1820–1830. The portraits, from Vermont, were done by an unknown artist.*

"This is the ultimate way to enjoy antiques," says the owner, who finds his house "very exciting" and not the least bit sparse or museumlike. "In a period setting," he adds, "all the objects blend together and you don't appreciate individual pieces as you do here." The problem, he admits, is in selecting only the items you can use and have space to properly display, an especially hard task for collectors.

This house is a lesson for those who appreciate the craftsmanship of the past, and also enjoy modern architecture and convenience. In blending the two, each enhances the other.

27

Connecticut highboy, *c. 1760, has been preserved in its original state.*

28

J. BARRY O'ROURKE

FACELIFT FOR A FORGE

Designer John Saladino and his wife, Virginia, are serious collectors of American antiques. But they felt that their converted, 18th-century forge needed more than primitive furnishings. Their choice was comfortable Saladino-designed leather sofas and lighting that enhance the old woods.

Old bellows, *hung between the fireplace flues, is a reminder that this house was once a working forge.*

Unframed, *see-through screening, attached to sapling supports, opens the porch to nature.*

Antique lighting *fixtures and candle holders from the Saladinos' collection blend with modern lamps. Oval hutch table, chairs, and settle are 18th century.*

THE COUNTRY STORE

The merchandise in this New England general store is not for sale. It belongs, rather, to a private collection of 19th-century "country store paraphernalia," housed in what was, from 1825 to 1969, a functioning shop.

"General store" contains late 19th-century merchandise and advertising displays collected over fifteen years.

The owners, who live upstairs in the country-style Greek Revival building, did not plan to display their collection in this manner when they bought this house six years ago. They had been collecting canisters, advertising displays, bandboxes, and other 19th-century dry goods at tag sales, flea markets, antiques and junk shops for years because they were "colorful, interesting, and, when we started, inexpensive." As they unpacked, however, they would "temporarily" put items on the old store shelves. Friends and relatives would also donate merchandise they thought was appropriate, and, eventually, the "fantasy, make-believe land" took shape.

The shop is arranged in departments: tea and coffee, ladies' wear, men's wear, fabric, and so on. It is a favorite space for entertaining, and it is not unusual for party guests to dress up in the old clothes the owners have placed "on sale" in the store.

Upstairs in the living quarters, the mood is very different. Here the furnishings are much older and finer—18th- and early 19th-century painted furniture, fine blown glassware, and fragile antique pottery.

Penny candy *in authentic 19th-century glass jars is always on hand for "customers" of the general store.*

Fabric bolts *in the "sewing department" are actually small pieces of antique textiles wrapped around empty fabric rolls. Collections of antique canisters, china, pottery, lanterns, and toys were bought one at a time at tag sales, flea markets, and junk and antiques shops. Display cases and furniture in the store are all authentic 19th-century pieces.*

32

NEW MEXICAN HERITAGE

Casa San Ysidro, the Corrales, N. Mex., home of Alan and Shirley Minge, was an unwanted ruin when the Minges bought it in 1950. In rebuilding the adobe house, they found the foundations of a much larger building behind it, which the owners believe were the remains of an 18th-century Spanish colonial hacienda.

The Minges have restored the twenty-two-room hacienda as accurately as possible, searching out, over the last thirty years, New Mexican architectural fragments, tools, furniture, artwork, and even outbuildings to move to the site. Today, the house, built around a central courtyard, is a standing record of the grandest type of 18th-century domestic architecture in New Mexico.

The weaving room, shown here, contains a massive horizontal pine loom, c. 1775, that was made in the Española region of New Mexico. It is still operable, and is the type of machine that was used to weave antique *jergas*, woolen carpets made from handwoven strips sewn together, that are shown below.

Pine loom, *used to weave* jergas, *was made in New Mexico about 1775. It is still in working condition.*

Blanket pole *holds a collection of antique* jergas, *carpets made from handwoven woolen strips.*

33

34

THE COUNTRY FASHION

"Collecting has always been a passion," says fashion designer Bill Blass, who was buying antiques long before he bought this house, an 18th-century New England stone tavern. On his frequent travels around the world, Blass enjoys searching for antique furniture, as well as porcelain, wooden animals, or anything else that is his favorite collectible at the moment. Before he moved here, he was mainly interested in English antiques, but now, living in the heart of New England, he collects American pieces as well.

But it is the house itself that has essentially determined its decoration. "I'm so fond of this house that I try to keep what I put in from intruding on its good looks," says Blass. The living room, for example, is a sparsely furnished, subdued space with white walls, quiet print fabrics, and a fine, but not overpowering, collection of international antiques. A large room with two fireplaces, it was created by joining the two waiting rooms—one for men, one for women—of the original tavern.

And because he is so fond of the views of the New England countryside, windows in the downstairs rooms are curtainless.

Audubon paintings *hang over the living-room fireplaces. An Italian flag cabinet stands between the windows.*

FRANK KOLLEOGY

Mud room's table *is Scottish; shelf is Mexican; baskets are international.*

FRANK KOLLEOGY

Wing chair, *covered with a French quilt, is 18th-century American.*

CHRIS MEAD

THE COUNTRY MOVES WEST

For many people "country" is a term applied to New England keeping rooms, Pennsylvania stone kitchens, and Virginia herb gardens—images commonly associated with the Early American colonies. But as Americans moved west, the "country" moved west too, and people adopted what they found into their homes and their way of living.

Today, Indian pottery and blankets are just as important for the country house as New England stoneware and Amish quilts, and Spanish *santos* and Indian kachinas of the Southwest are as valued in American folk art as weather vanes and whirligigs.

In the West, particularly, there is still the opportunity to appreciate the colors, the textures, even the aromas of wide-open land and sky, to see how these elements can be incorporated into the home. In short, you bring the country into your house by using what is native to the land, both culturally and naturally.

Horse barn, *suited to the wide-open spaces of Wyoming, is one of the early building forms of the American West.*

CHRIS MEAD

Weathered wood, *natural objects, grass, and snow combine for a rustic motif. These are some of the colors and textures country decorating brings to a home.*

38

THE SHAKER WAY

The Shakers arrived in America in 1774 with only eight members. Mother Ann Lee, the leader of this branch of the Quaker religion, preached a Utopian gospel of sinlessness and celibacy. In their search for new converts, Shaker missionaries traveled as far from their original settlement in New York State as Kentucky, where, in 1805, three Mercer County farmers adopted the Shaker faith and founded the Pleasant Hill Shaker community. By 1820 Pleasant Hill was almost entirely self-sufficient, boasting 500 members, flourishing crops, and thriving businesses.

Pleasant Hill's last twelve Believers left in 1910, but in 1961 the property was privately acquired, and is today a nonprofit institution known as Shaker Village. Visitors can walk through the restored Shaker buildings and watch craftsmen in Shaker dress practicing traditional crafts. The dining room serves simple Shaker fare, and rooms are available.

Hand-tooled limestone, *known locally as white marble, was used to build the "Old Stone Shop" and walk.*

"Old Stone Shop" *was originally built in 1811 as a Shaker dwelling and later served as a shop.*

COUNTRY IN THE CITY

The furniture made for the sophisticated urban markets of the past—Boston, Newport, New York, Philadelphia, Baltimore, Charleston—differed significantly from the serviceable, sturdy, but unpretentious pieces made by country cabinetmakers for their rural customers. While city artisans copied from the latest European pattern books, decorated their work with ornate carvings and fancy details, and used valuable woods such as mahogany, the country craftsman made simplified versions of chests, tables, chairs, and worked in pine and other common woods, often painted to imitate the more expensive varieties.

City apartment *is decorated with contemporary seating as well as antique country furnishings: stripped pine mantel, pine tables, and closed cupboard.*

Today, those country furnishings, once scorned by wealthy city residents, decorate houses and apartments in the best urban neighborhoods. And where urban dwellers once accessorized their houses with fine European ceramics and fabrics, and rugs from the Orient, many now accent their country pieces with salt-glazed stoneware, homespun fabrics and handmade quilts, rag rugs, and other unpretentious items.

41

Country accessories *in a New York City den include a "Feathered Star" quilt, c. 1855, on the wall, quilt remnant pillows, antique birdhouse.*

LIFE OVER THE STORE

George E. Schoellkopf, collector, dealer, and authority on Americana, lives over his store, a gallery of antiques and folk art, in a Manhattan brownstone. His apartment, designed by Harry M. Schule and Ned R. Marshall, combines a neutral-toned, contemporary-style background with Schoellkopf's collection of paintings, sculpture, pottery, textiles, and country furniture, all spotlighted from tracks above. The folk art and furniture are of the finest quality in keeping with Schoellkopf's philosophy that while less-than-perfect pieces can be used successfully in charming old houses, only the best will work with stark modern decors.

Hooked rug, *c. 1880, commemorates the exploits of a family pet.*
Eagle *(right) was carved in Pennsylvania in the late 19th century by Wilhelm Schimmel.*

Redware and slipware *from early- to mid-19th-century Pennsylvania and New England are exhibited in the built-in bookcases.*

Painted cupboard, *c. 1750, holds redware and a "bottle doll" doorstop.*

Wood carvings *of Quakers (a symbol of honesty) once stood in a store.*

CITY SLICKER

George E. Schoellkopf has been collecting antiques since childhood, but he has been specializing in Americana in recent years, ever since he moved to New York to study art history. His apartment is filled with his collections of folk art and country furniture set against a neutral taupe background.

Checkerboards *(right) are mid- to late-19th century; painted side chair dates c. 1790.*

44

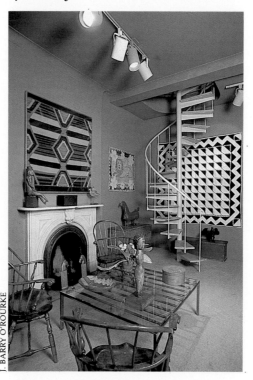

Carved chest, *c. 1820, is from Salem, Mass. Weather vane above was made c. 1870.*

"Kansas Troubles" *quilt dates c. 1900. A Navaho child's blanket is over the mantel.*

Mammy doll *with leather feet and arms, c. 1850, sits in a Windsor highchair.*

PARADISE IN THE CITY

For Tom Pritchard and William Jarecki, two of the partners in Manhattan's exotic plant shop, Mädderlake, their garden is a natural extension of their work. And it was an important factor in their decision to buy their apartment, the ground floor of an 1827 Federal-style row house in Greenwich Village.

Both the garden and the apartment were in bad condition when the two men bought the property. They totally gutted the interior, and then rebuilt it in stages. The greenhouse shown here was originally constructed as a winter home for tropical potted plants that summered in the garden. But the plants were eventually moved to the shop, and when the kitchen was enlarged to take over part of the bedroom, the large platform bed was moved to the greenhouse "temporarily." It is such a pleasant spot for sleeping that it became the permanent bedroom.

The garden was an unexciting

*"**Flower Garden**"quilt, made by an Ohio Amish woman in 1920, covers the bed in the greenhouse bedroom. Foliage outside provides privacy.*

expanse of ivy surrounded by a concrete walk before Pritchard and Jarecki moved in. Today it is a multileveled tropical paradise, complete with a small recirculating pool and a hammock for relaxing. Since it does not get much sun, the area is more suited to fan palms, antherium, philodendron, and other tropical greens than to most flowering plants. Many plants are potted so they can be moved when entertaining and to create different arrangements. Mossy brick and ivy ground cover help keep the atmosphere moist and cool, and different levels increase both the number of plants and the number of people the space can hold for entertaining. The whole exemplifies the owners' philosophy that "designing a city garden or terrace is more than simply setting out potted plants: It involves modulating space and cultivating views too."

Through their garden, these two men have brought the country into the city. And by physically opening their house to the garden, they have brought the country indoors as well.

Multileveled terraces *increase both the number of plants and people this city garden can hold. Most plants are tropical greens; the ground cover is ivy.*

FRANK KOLLEOGY

FUNDAMENTAL FOLK ART

Robert Bishop, director of New York City's Museum of American Folk Art, grew up in the antiques business. "My grandmother was an antiques dealer in Maine," he mentions. "I opened my first shop and bought my first antique—a Newport, R.I., Queen Anne chair by John Goddard—when I was 13." He paid $18 for the chair, and later sold it for $650.

The renovated 1850s town house in New York's Chelsea district where Dr. Bishop lives today was a run-down rooming house with 16 tenants when he bought it. He gutted the building, turned it into two duplex apartments, and filled his space with his extensive collections of Shaker furniture and antique and contemporary American folk art. The folk art display, which covers practically all available wall and surface space, constantly changes as different pieces are loaned to museums throughout the world.

Shaker chairs *from the Mount Lebanon community stand beside a Kentucky Shaker worktable and a New York Shaker candlestand.*

48

Weather vane *still retains the painted dial that told wind direction.*

Dr. Bishop adds to his collections on the basis of quality, buying only the best available, whatever the category—furniture, painting, sculpture, textiles. As is evidenced by his home, folk painting is a special interest. His favorite contemporary folk artists are Mattie Lou O'Kelley, who painted the magenta and pink flowers on a black background hanging on the art-covered wall at left, and Kathie Jakobsen. Ms. Jakobsen's portrayals of *The Shaker Barn* and a *New York State Scene*, a city street, also hang on the wall.

All the furniture shown in this living room is Shaker, including the daybed.

Shaker daybed *and cupboard stand beneath a constantly changing display of contemporary folk paintings.*

49

II

P A R T II

COUNTRY ROOMS

53

The houses of the earliest American settlers had but one or two multipurpose rooms, which were filled with equally multipurpose furnishings: settle beds, chair-tables, storage chests. As the colonists prospered, the houses grew larger, with rooms added for the specific purposes of eating, sleeping, and entertaining. Country is a decorating style that works for all these rooms in your house or apartment, from the living room to the bath.

Presented here are both the basic components of rooms—simple tables, chairs, cupboards, beds, and other important pieces of furniture—and examples of how these components have been successfully combined for rooms with a country look. The spaces show country pieces blended with modern furnishings and appliances, as well as more traditional interiors that have been decorated with a combination of antiques and reproductions.

LIVING ROOMS

The living room, as we think of it today, is a relatively modern concept, and one that changes in meaning according to the size of your house or apartment and the ways in which your rooms are used. In small houses and apartments (especially studio apartments), the living room is more like the "hall" of early colonial days, a term derived from England and applied to the general utility room used for cooking, dining, living, and sleeping. In larger living quarters, with separate dens, dining rooms, and playrooms, the living room is a more formal space, more like the "parlor" was in the past—a room furnished with the best pieces the family owned (often including their prized bedstead), and used for receiving the clergy and other important guests.

But few people today would find antique parlor furniture comfortable. Most of the rooms shown here, therefore, combine handsome, well-upholstered contemporary pieces with antiques, folk art, and country accessories used for accent and to create a relaxed, welcoming atmosphere.

Gateleg table *in this Virginia living room is 18th century; the country settee is from the early 20th century.*

Crib quilt *in a "One Patch" pattern, c. 1840, and an Indiana quilt in an original design, c. 1890, are hung as artwork in a California house.*

55

ROBERT SCHENKER

MANTELS

The fireplace mantel is a fine spot to display your favorite objects and collections. Suit the choice of objects and the arrangement to the room. A spare, symmetrical display works best in very formal parlors and living rooms and lends importance to the objects on view. Less formal arrangements of collectibles are more suited to casually decorated rooms. Change these displays when you feel the mood or to suit the season.

56

Watermelon slice *by folk artist Miles Carpenter and contemporary carvings sit on a c. 1800 mantel.*

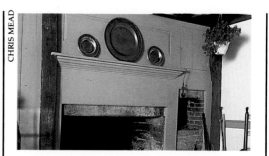

Pewter plates *from the 18th century form a symmetrical arrangement.*

Cloth ornaments *made from quilt pieces during quilting bees decorate this mantel.*

Antique toys *grace the 1750 mantel of a Connecticut farmhouse. Most of the toys are 19th-century American, including the papier-mâché rooster, the chalk rabbit, and the drum and horns.*

Herb wreath *hangs above a simple mantel. The drying rack is Shaker.*

Spongewear pitchers, *plates hand painted by Jeanne Nastav, and antique candlesticks top a pine mantel.*

Pewter plates, *tankards, and candlesticks decorate a mantel made from an old wood beam. Antique wrought-iron fireplace utensils hang from the mantel. Portraits on either side are of ancestors of Daniel Webster.*

57

Toleware mugs *and pitchers are lined up beneath an oil painting by R. W. and S. A. Shute.*

Civil War sword *(from the North) hangs on the original mantel of a renovated 18th-century tavern. Above are English watercolors and American decoys.*

Slipcovers *made of "Castle" fabric by Stroheim & Romann cover a comfortable sofa by Swaim Originals. On top are quilt remnant pillows from the shop at the Museum of American Folk Art. Antique hand-painted plates hanging above the sofa are from Portugal.*

58

Platform seating, *shown here as a sofa, was purposely made wide enough to double as a sleeping unit. Fabrics for cushions, designed by Gear for Cohama/ Riverdale, are in "Rust" and "Barn Rose" colors. Antique rag rug is from Pennsylvania.*

CHAIRS AND SOFAS

A seat or bed—the forerunner of modern couches—placed near the kitchen hearth was a country tradition in Early America. But the hard settles, benches, and chairs of those days cannot provide the comfort of today's upholstered seating. And handsome contemporary pieces, whether covered in a solid color or print, blend well with the antiques and accessories that set the mood in the country living room.

Doll-sized twig *rocker has pillows made from antique quilt pieces.*

"Country Basket" *fabric, in "Rust" colorway, from the New Country Gear collection for Cohama/Riverdale Decorative Fabrics, covers a contemporary sofa. Coordinating pillows, made by Riverdale Pillow, are in "Checks and Stripes" and "Country Daisy" patterns in "Midnight" and "Stone Blue" tones, as well as "Country Basket" for the duffel-style pillow. Fabrics cost approximately $8.50 to $9 per yard.*

White piqué *fabric, with antimacassar trim, covers a new chair.*

Daybed, *or child's bed, with rope supports, was made in Pennsylvania c. 1850. Now used as a sofa, it is covered with a 19th-century New England quilt and pillows made from quilt pieces.*

Wicker sofa, *a clean-lined, contemporary piece, becomes a bed when this porch is used for sleeping in the summer months.*

PRESERVING THE PAST

Because of their great respect for the past and their love of the solid, handcrafted Texas houses of the last century, Beverly and Tommy Jacomini have gone to great lengths to maintain the authenticity and integrity of their 1857 farmhouse. The air-conditioning system, for example, has been installed so that it is practically invisible, with no units or vents in view to mar the house's past-century atmosphere. The mantel in the living room, shown here, was totally reconstructed from old wood to closely resemble the original. And rather than build closets in a house where none existed, the Jacominis use large armoires and the under-eaves spaces for storage.

Furnishings are in keeping with this feeling for the past. Most are antique, and many pieces were made on the old Texas homesteads. The decor is relaxed and inviting, a place where children and dogs can roam without worrying about harming the furnishings or the house.

Blanket chest *is a Texas antique. A framed crazy quilt hangs on the wall.* **Sleigh bed,** *made in Texas in the last century, is used as a sofa. Pillows were made from pieces of old quilts.*

60

61

FARMHOUSE FLAVOR

While the architecture of Mr. and Mrs. Sanford McCormick's house in the Texas countryside is strikingly contemporary, the building echoes, in its plan, materials, and ambience, the "typical old Texas farmhouse" it replaced on this beautiful pastoral site.

The McCormicks had worked with architect W. Irving Philips, Jr., on a number of previous projects, including the renovation of the farmhouse that stood here until destroyed by fire. Together, architect and owners planned a house that Balene McCormick calls "eclectic in its concept." The large open living room shown here, with its stone walls and bare wood floors, is reminiscent of the original farmhouse, while the paved courtyard in front of the house gives evidence of the Spanish influence in Texas.

Pennsylvania quilt *hangs behind contemporary sofas. On the wall at left is a French blacksmith's sign.*

62

CHRIS MEAD

CHRIS MEAD

Furnishings, too, are a mix of styles and periods, with an emphasis on "the primitive approach," explains Balene. For the past 20 years, the McCormicks have collected "unsophisticated art" wherever they have traveled: workmen's tools in France; pre-Columbian art in Mexico; baskets and American Indian blankets in California and throughout the West; tramp art, quilts, and other folk art and primitive furniture on the East Coast. They also collect native Texas pieces, such as the quilt and bench shown below.

Workmen's tools *are predominantly French, found in Paris and the surrounding countryside. Included in the collection are implements used by masons, blacksmiths, and farmers. The boot signs, spinning wheel, and windmill weight shaped like a man are American.*

Tramp art chest *was made from mahogany cigar boxes at the turn of the 20th century. Tramp art was created from the 1860s to the 1920s by layering wood from cigar or fruit boxes, then chip carving.*

Mirror frames, *a common form of tramp art, were made by craftsmen in the East and Southwest in the late 19th and early 20th centuries.*

Mission bench *was made in San Antonio, c. 1850. Antique "friendship" quilt top was made from individually sewn squares.*

WIDE OPEN SPACES

Designer Raymond Waites and his wife, Nancy, bought their East Hampton, N.Y., cottage for its close-to-the-beach location, then tore down the interior walls to create a large open area for living, dining, and sleeping. Only white and pale wood tones have been used, a backdrop that allows simple objects to be seen as sculpture.

Fabrics *were inspired by rustic motifs and colors from nature.*

Glass doors *(left) make the woods outside a part of the room's design.*

"Living island," *centered in the large room, contains storage for stereo equipment, a plug for the telephone, and a display top for objects.*

AN ACQUIRED TASTE

"We're acquisitive people," say Helaine and Burton Fendelman. "Our collections have bred collections." In fact, the Fendelmans bought their 1850 farmhouse in suburban New York when they collected themselves out of a city apartment after two years of buying. They started acquiring old things because they wanted a distinctive, personal look in their house. Now they buy "whatever we like and have money and room for," especially painted and decorated furniture. Their collection, however, is not haphazard: each piece is carefully chosen.

Shooting gallery targets, *made of cast iron, are an early 20th-century folk art form. Because it is painted, the duck, second from right, is especially rare.*

Folk art turkey *was carved by contemporary artist Felipe Archuleta.*

Painted chest *from 19th-century New England is the center of a grouping of folk art in the living room. The sofa is also 19th-century New England.*

TEXTILES TO TREASURE

Every room of Barbara and Mel Ohrbach's converted 1925 carriage house is furnished around an antique textile. The Ohrbachs' love for old fabrics, rugs, and quilts stems from Barbara's fashion background; and their New York City shop, Cherchez, where they specialize in old textiles, is an extension of that interest. The living room shown here was designed around the old Aubusson rug. Victorian wicker furniture was painted khaki to blend with the rug, and the cushions were covered with French butcher's smock fabric.

Old fireboards *are hard to find, so Barbara Ohrbach painted this one herself. The twig rockers are Victorian.*

CHRIS MEAD

Oversized basket *on the wall is a southern antique, once used for drying large tobacco leaves. Blanket chest, now a coffee table, is a 19th-century New England piece, as is the blue-painted washstand.*

WINTER INTO SUMMER

The Emmerling apartment had not been altered for almost 50 years, since the building's construction in 1928, when we bought it three years ago. As in many older New York City buildings, the rooms are large with high ceilings, and, especially in the living room shown here, very little had to be done to make it the perfect home for our two children and the American primitive furnishings we have collected over the past 10 years.

The living-room walls are painted white and the wood floors left bare to provide a neutral background for the warm wood tones

68

and subtly painted colors of the antique furnishings. Contemporary sofas and lamps also complement, but do not compete with, the antiques and folk art that give the apartment its personality. The original fireplace mantel was out of scale with the room and was replaced with an antique pine mantel.

To keep the interiors interesting, I occasionally change the accessories, move the furniture to different rooms, and slipcover the living-room sofas. In the winter the sofas are plain white. Accessories are mainly bright red and green. In the summer I switch to blue-and-white check slipcovers, with pastel accents. A painting replaces a basket on the far wall, a checkerboard changes places with a wreath above the fireplace, one quilt is switched for another, and, with no expense (after the initial cost of the slipcovers), I have a living room with a new look.

Stoneware crocks, *planted with geraniums, line the windowsill (above). An antique dhurrie rug is on the floor.*
White sofas *are accented with pillows from the shop of the Museum of American Folk Art (above right).*
Pine mantel, *c. 1800, is decorated in winter with a watermelon carving by Miles Carpenter (right).*
Blue-and-white *checked slipcovers in "Castle" fabric by Stroheim & Romann and hot pink pillows give a fresh look in summer (left).*

69

POTTING SHED REBORN

The owners of this house, a renovated mid-19th-century Connecticut potting shed with a 20-year-old addition, love antique furniture. They also love comfortable contemporary seating and practical modern lighting. To combine their interests, they hired interior designer John Saladino, who helped them both restructure and decorate their house.

First, Saladino gutted the interior of the entire house. In the living room, shown here, he took down the low ceiling, exposing the framework above, and opened the space with skylights and sliding glass doors. Opposite these are the sliding barn doors seen here, made from siding taken from an old barn on the property.

In each room Saladino then mixed new furnishings with the owners' collection of antiques, creating an atmosphere that is bright, contemporary, and, at the same time, cozy. Here, custom sofas and Saladino-designed lighting blend with antiques.

Breadbasket (*above*) *holds a stoneware pitcher and wooden candlesticks.*

Barn doors *and a newly opened ceiling framework help this addition (opposite) blend with the original house.*

Pennsylvania Dutch cupboard *has its old rattail hinges.*

71

FOLK ART FANTASYLAND

Jeffrey Camp, the proprietor, with his wife, Jane, of the American Folk Art Company in Tappahannock, Va., discovered contemporary folk art while searching rural areas for traditional crafts. Today he deals exclusively in modern folk paintings and carvings, which he combines in his house with antique furniture.

Folk carvings *by Miles Carpenter, modern paintings, and rattan chairs furnish the living room.*

Eli Whitney, *painted by Reverend Howard Finster, hangs beside Finster's church carving.*

73

Fantastic figures *are all products of the vivid imagination of 90-year-old Virginia folk artist Miles Carpenter.*

DENS AND FAMILY ROOMS

Early American houses had few rooms, and each had to serve many purposes. It was common for a family to cook, eat, and sleep in one large fireplace-warmed space—the original family room. Over the years houses grew larger and rooms developed more specific functions. In these days of many-roomed houses (and central heating), the family is less apt to gather around the kitchen stove than the den or family room television set.

In houses with formal living rooms, the den has become an informal spot for relaxing and entertaining. The furnishings you choose for this space should reflect that informality, and almost all primitive country pieces do.

Antiques *from England and America, including an 18th-century Virginia wing chair, covered with an old wool blanket, decorate a Virginia library.*

Multipurpose furnishings are especially well suited to rooms that are the center of a family's varied activities. A dry sink, for example, can function simultaneously as a bar and stereo cabinet. Benches can be used for seating, storage, or for displaying accessories.

Because there is no direct counterpart of the den in rural Early American houses, even purists need not feel constrained to furnish the space authentically: TVs, hi-fis, comfortable contemporary seating and lighting, and other accouterments of modern living will blend perfectly with your primitive country furnishings.

75

One-room cabin, *part of the Shelburne Museum in Vermont, is made of dovetailed logs and contains benches hewn from logs and a "laundry corner" with ironbound wooden tub.*

CHRIS MEAD

Squares, diamonds, *and cubes, designed to simulate mosaic tile pavement, were popular patterns for both painted floors and floorcloths in Early American country houses. The painting was usually done by itinerant artists who also grained the woodwork and decorated the walls with stenciled or freehand designs.* **Wide-board floor** *in the kitchen of the "Stencil House" in Vermont's Shelburne Museum is painted green. Painted floors—both plain and patterned—were popular in colonial times since worn spots could be easily repaired at minimum expense. If you are painting a floor today, protect the color or decoration with several coats of clear shellac.*

76

FLOOR COVERINGS

Most American floors were bare in the 17th and early 18th centuries. Carpets were rare and valuable and used as table coverings. But by the mid-18th century, carpets were being used on floors by those who could afford them, floors and canvas fabrics were being painted to imitate expensive woven carpets, tiles, and parquet. Hand-woven striped carpets, homemade rag rugs, straw matting, and braided and hooked rugs also became popular in country households after 1800.

Contemporary rag rugs *are available at Marimekko stores.*

HOOKED RUGS

The hooked rug served a dual purpose in the 19th- and early 20th-century house: It covered the floor and efficiently recycled worn, but still precious, pieces of cloth. The best craftsmen combined an innate sense of color and design with their ability to hook loops of material—yarn or wool rags cut into strips—through the holes of a coarsely woven ground fabric (most commonly burlap) to form a pile. The result is a charming folk art form and today collecting hooked rugs is very popular.

Most hooked rugs now available were made between 1850 and 1930, but the exact age of a rug is difficult to determine. After 1870, there were many rugs in the same design when printed patterns became common, but rugs that vary from a set pattern or are unusual in shape or size are naturally more valuable. Among rug designs, pictorial rugs are now more valuable than floral or geometric patterns. Whatever the type, a rug must be in good condition to be worth buying as a floor covering or a wall hanging.

Flowerpot *with stylized designs is made of wool strips on burlap.*

Pennsylvania hooked rug *with chickens was made c. 1860.*

Landscape rug *from the 19th century has a charming, design.*

White horse *on a starburst ground is a mid-19th-century rug.*

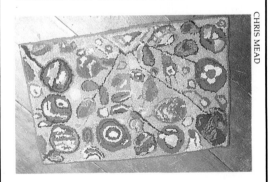

Floral motif, *an abstract pattern, may have been hand drawn.*

Common animals—*cats, dogs, horses—were popular rug patterns.*

Corner hearts *add a personal touch to a stylized New England floral rug.*

Reindeer *is a striking and unusual form on a New England hooked rug.*

77

CHRIS MEAD

Church pews, *backless to keep the congregation awake, stand in an 1840 church in the Museum of Appalachia. Pews were made of split logs of poplar.*

78

J. BARRY O'ROURKE

Windsor settee *was made in Connecticut, c. 1850. On the bench are a "Buster Brown" doll, c. 1900, and antique and contemporary rag dolls.*

BENCHES

Simple stools and benches are possibly the world's oldest seats. In Early America these primitive wooden forms were used in barns for milking, in schools and meetinghouses, in carpenters' and cobblers' workshops, and for many household tasks.

Decorative bench, *a collapsible piece that is now a garden ornament, might have stood in a railroad station at the turn of the century.*

Child's settle, *made in 19th-century New England, was painted to imitate wood graining.*

Pine bench *with oak legs was made in New Mexico in the 19th century. Pueblo Indian pottery, an array of New Mexican pieces dating from the 18th to the 20th centuries, is displayed on top.*

Footstool, *painted blue and made c. 1890, is owned by antiques dealer Corinne Burke, who uses this and similar pieces as display stands throughout her house.*

CUPBOARDS AND BLANKET CHESTS

Blanket chests and cupboards were essential pieces of furniture in the Early American house because closets were nonexistent.

Chests are simply boxes, with or without legs and feet, and with a hinged lid. The simplest form is the "six-board" chest, which takes its name from the number of pieces of wood it took to build

Pine cupboard, *c. 1780, is a country version of the Dutch* kas. *The Long Island piece has ball feet. Hooked rug above is from New England.*

one. These were made from 1700 on, and the more valuable ones were painted. Especially valuable are the elaborately decorated dower chests.

Cupboards evolved from chests and were originally built into the walls of houses. They were almost always painted.

Standing cupboard, *made of pine and painted red, is an 18th-century Connecticut antique now used to store bed linens and clothes. Three old baskets are displayed on top—the middle one is a Shaker broom basket. Small ladder-back child's chair and the unframed samplers above it are all from 18th-century New England.*

Green-painted *cupboard from 18th-century Rhode Island now provides storage space in a city apartment. Old peg rack alongside holds accessories.*

Pine chest, *c. 1750, still has its original red paint. The small hanging cupboard above the blanket chest is from 18th-century New Hampshire.*

Blanket chest, *embellished with hearts and other folk art motifs, was made in 18th-century Pennsylvania.*

81

Country cupboard, *a primitive southern piece, holds homemade soaps.*

Pine chest *was made c. 1725 in Lowell, Mass. Paint is all original.*

Canadian cupboard, *made in the 18th century, had its doors removed at some time in the past. Today it stores antique herb containers and quilts and coverlets for the bed.*

Nautical memorabilia *collected by Richard Haders—the 1889 painting by Antonio Jacobsen, the ship weather vane—are reminders of New England's seagoing past. Blue-and-white bowls on the coffee table are part of Phyllis Haders' collection of c. 1830–1840 spongeware.*

FOLK ART POTPOURRI

"Our collection is eclectic," says Phyllis Haders. "I'm not at all a purist—I buy anything that makes me feel good." Folk art in the Haders' house is international, from small, hand-carved whales to a wooden African lion to contemporary American paintings.

Baby-sized quilt, *"Robbing Peter to Pay Paul," framed in plexiglass, hangs above a 1920s whirligig.*

Apothecary chest *is a refinished Massachusetts piece.*

TO THE MANOR BORN

"Big Bend Farm," George Weymouth's house at the big bend of the Brandywine River in Pennsylvania, started as a two-room cottage in the 1680s on land sold to William Penn by the chief of the Lenni Lenape Indians. Lo-

Pennsylvania settle, c. 1710, and wing chair with unusual rush seat are in the "sitting" end of the room. Antique redware above settle is part of service for 30.

cal legend says that the house was used as a trading post, and that in 1763 it became the foundation for the Queen Anne manor house a Scottish captain built for his mistress. The stone house was abandoned when Weymouth, chairman of the board of the Brandywine Conservancy and a painter himself, bought it almost twenty years ago. It was lovingly, carefully restored to its Queen Anne style (a three-and-a-half-year process) and furnished with small scale antiques of the period to fit the small size of most of the rooms. Shown here is the old summer kitchen—the original two-room house—now serving a new role as a sitting/dining room.

Red-brick floor *and white walls effectively set off the textures of old baskets and wood. Almost all the furnishings in the house are early 18th century.*

CHRIS MEAD

HOOKED ON RUGS

When the owners of this 1750 Connecticut farmhouse decided to enlarge their house with materials from an even older house, they chose not to be constrained by 18th-century architecture. Using old boards, beams, and shingles, as well as antiques dating from 1720 to 1830, they created two spacious rooms that retain the feeling, though not the structure, of the past. In every room 19th-century hooked rugs are prominently displayed.

Blanket chest *with ovoid feet, c. 1720, is a red-painted New England antique. Only two drawers actually open—the others are just for show.*

Hooked rugs *in floral patterns are used on wall and floor in the "Stencil Room." Both rugs are mid-19th century. White-painted Federal table still shows its original decoration.*

Child-sized grain-painted settle *of the 19th-century and an early 19th-century hutch table in rare orange paint face the fire in the keeping room. A mid-19th-century hooked rug hangs above.*

86

CHRIS MEAD

BEDROOMS

The earliest American houses had no bedrooms. People slept either in wood-framed units, called jack beds, that were built into the wall, or in rough-hewn, freestanding beds in the main room. By the 18th century, however, the bed disappeared from the great hall or parlor and became the center of a separate room.

Early American country bedrooms (or chambers, as they were called) were not the comfortable spaces we know today. Away from the kitchen fire, they were often cold and drafty. Mattresses were stuffed with corn husks or other uncomfortable fillings, and sat on rope supports.

Today the bedroom should be your private retreat, as comfortable and restful as possible. Al-

Four-poster bed *was made from discarded fishermen's trap stakes, trunks of young pines cut to support fish nets. Quilts are from the 19th century.*

ROBERT PERRON

Country accessories—*an antique patchwork quilt, a folk art still-life painting—bring warmth, color, and pattern to a contemporary bedroom.*

though authentic Early American beds are rare and expensive, and often too small for modern tastes, a number of firms make good reproductions in the country mood. And even if your bed is a plain metal frame or a contemporary platform, the quilts, coverlets, rag rugs, and other accessories you surround it with will supply the warm, welcoming country ambience.

89

J. BARRY O'ROURKE

LIGHTING DEVICES

Most artificial light in the Early American house came from the fireplace. Candle holders and sconces, lanterns and oil-burning lamps provided some illumination, but now we must consider these antiques mainly as decorative accessories. More suited to today's country places are modern lamps in simple earthenware shapes or unobtrusive metal forms that blend well with the objects of the past while supplying adequate light. And for atmosphere, a number of firms make fine reproductions.

CHRIS MEAD

Dramatic light *comes from a cymbal, suspended from the ceiling with transparent cord, that reflects the light shined into it by a floor can. This example of "light through indirection" was designed by John Saladino.*

Spotlight, *plugged into a track placed between ceiling beams, provides efficient task lighting.*

"Radio Wave" light *by Abolite hangs over a kitchen table.*

Kerosene lantern *is a decorative accessory that can still be used.*

Lantern, *now electrified, burned kerosene in the late 19th century.*

Reproduction chandelier, *a copy of an early New England form, is made with turned wood shafts, painted red, and wire arms. Reproductions of Early American lighting forms are made by Gates Moore, Norwalk, Conn., and Authentic Designs in New York City.*

91

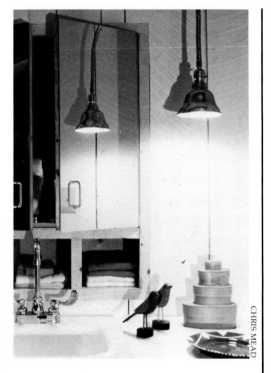

Work light, *an inexpensive, industrial-style piece, attaches to the wall.*

Stoneware jar *from England, c. 1850, is now the base of a table lamp.*

WALL TREATMENTS

While the earliest American houses had bare wood walls, later generations favored paneling, colorful paint, painted imitations of marble and wood grains, decorative stencils, and, when it could be afforded, wallpaper. Today, you can decorate your walls yourself, or hire specialized craftsmen.

"Wash Bluing" walls *in a log cabin at Henkel Square Museum in Texas were created by adding bleach to paint.*

Stone wall *was chosen for the interior of a converted barn in Pennsylvania, where stone is a traditional building material.*

Wood wall, *part of an enclosed porch, was purposely left uninsulated and unpainted so the owner could enjoy the rustic look of the rough cedar shingles.*

92

Stencil border *was painted in 1857 by a German immigrant to Texas.*

Wall coverings *from Imperial include "Country Daisy" (below), "Country Basket" (right).*

93

PEG RACKS

Closets were practically nonexistent in Early American houses. Pegs, peg racks, blanket and towel racks were necessities, therefore, for keeping clothing and household articles orderly. Some of the most beautiful racks were made by the Shakers to hold everything from embroidered towels to chairs to bonnets.

Children's wear *of the 19th century hangs from a standing clothes rack (with trestle feet) of the same period.*

94

Garden rake head (*above*) *is used as an accessory rack in a bedroom. Although the pole has been removed here, the whole rake can be hung on your wall and used for odds and ends.*
Clothes rack *from the 18th century, painted gray, holds antique clothing in Vermont's Shelburne Museum.*

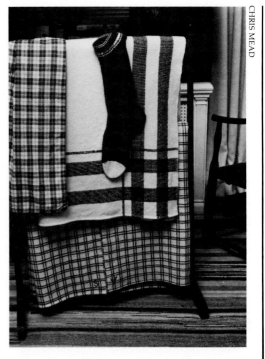

Hat racks *made of wood were once common sights in offices and stores, where they held visitors' outerwear. The 19th-century example below now stands in an apartment.*

Baseball caps *and other paraphernalia hang from a peg rack (above) in the bedroom of a young boy. Racks like this can be used in almost every room in the house.*

Blanket rack *from the 19th century holds homespun fabrics.*

Homespun blankets *were lowered on a pole to warm in front of the fire.*

Scrap bags, *old potholders, and herbs are displayed on peg rack (above).*

Drying plants, *antique baskets, and candles hang from old beam (below).*

SLEEPING LOFT

The conversion of this 200-year-old barn into living space was a "labor of love by four people," states Raymond Waites, the designer in charge of the project. Also involved in the remodeling were the barn's owners, William C. Musham and his wife, Bettye Martin, and contractor Rube Weaver, all of whom believe strongly in preserving the best of America's past, and in blending that heritage with the best of contemporary American design.

The results of their labors are seen here, the fourth level or sleeping loft of the barn, and in the introduction to this book. No unsightly air-conditioning units or elaborate heating systems mar the beautiful lines of the old structure. The center stone core of the barn is enclosed with Thermopane and heated by woodburning stoves. The other two-thirds of the space, including this loft high in the rafters, is left unheated in winter to cut energy consumption.

Inside, the decor is simple American Country, updated for a contemporary life-style. All the furnishings and fabrics were created by Gear Design, Inc. Furniture is clean lined and multipurpose. Fabrics are geometric, with a feeling of the past, but with patterns that are sparer, less flowery and fussy than antique textiles. Colors are basically monochromatic, easily mixed, and based on natural objects. And because of the desire to emphasize good American design, everything used in the house—from the industrial lamps to the kitchen appliances—was made in America.

Fourth-level loft *is an extra guest room or a quiet spot for relaxing.*
Industrial spot *clamps onto headboard to provide reading light. Fabric is new but with an old-fashioned feel.*

Stacked pillows, *easily rearranged, form the sleeping/lounging surface in the loft. Formica bench behind the pillows is a combination headboard and storage space. Lighting throughout the barn is industrial-style spots and candles.*

KEYSTONE COTTAGE

Pennsylvania interior designer and antiques dealer Harry Hartman admits that "antiques got into my bloodstream at an early age—I started at eight years old." He remembers that he "bought four rolls of Pennsylvania rag carpeting at an auction for 50¢, and used it until I was in my twenties. I still love old rag carpeting, although it is expensive and hard to find today."

Hartman's house is in keeping with his feelings for the past. It is a stone cottage built by Moravian settlers in 1778, and was later part of Linden Hall, the oldest girls' boarding school in the country. Hartman has restored the small "dollhouse" to its original condition. "Every piece of hardware in the place, except one, is authentic," he boasts, and even the windows have 18th-century glass.

All the furnishings in the house are antique, and most are of local Pennsylvania origin. Hartman's special love is American painted furniture, some outstanding examples of which are in the bedroom at right: Pennsylvania blanket chests, small boxes, hanging cupboard, and four-poster.

Four-poster bed, *made in Pennsylvania, c. 1800, is hung with homespun used by Mennonites to cover dry goods. Blanket chest is a 19th-century piece.*

Blanket chest, *c. 1800–1810, is painted in a style characteristic of Lebanon County, Pa. A stoneware jug and an antique grain-painted box rest on top.*

SOUTHERN HOSPITALITY

Guests at Pat and Jim Carter's Virginia home have the pleasure of sleeping in this beautiful bedroom, part of separate guest quarters that also include a small kitchen and bath. The four-poster bed was made of trap stakes, the trunks of young pine trees cut by local fishermen to hold their nets in the water. These stakes are discarded after a year. The bed is dressed with handwoven hangings and a 19th-century coverlet and the pillowcases are made from antique linen towels. An antique costumer holds clothes.

SENTIMENTAL STYLE

Kathy and John Schoemer's bedroom in their 1840 Connecticut house is decorated with a deeply personal assortment of valuable antiques, memorable keepsakes, and "practical" reproductions.

Kathy, a dealer in American country antiques, admits to a strong dislike for most reproductions, but, she says, "antique beds will not fit my husband, who is 6' 4", and authentic pencil-post beds and wing chairs are too expensive for everyday use." John's 18th-century cherry chest of drawers is a very fine antique, while Kathy sentimentally clings to her unpretentious Victorian cottage chest, "the first antique I ever bought."

Nantucket baskets *and a stoneware crock sit atop a pine cupboard.*

Pencil-post bed *appears refreshingly clean-lined without a canopy. Important accessories include old and new baskets, framed drawings by the Schoemers' son, and a collection of samplers.*

Warm tones *of brown, red, and yellow create a cozy mood. "Birds in Air" quilt on the wall and "Eight-Pointed Star" quilt on bed are both antique.*

QUICK-CHANGE QUILTS

As fast as I can change the quilts on the bed and wall, I can change the look of my bedroom. All the bedrooms in the Emmerling house have white backgrounds. Color and ambience come from the constantly varied selection of quilts, switched to suit the season or just my mood. Even my daughter, Samantha, has gotten into the quick-change act, frequently rearranging new and antique clothes on her doll-sized blanket rack.

Doll-sized blanket rack *holds Samantha's school clothes.*

Blue and white *is a crisp, fresh-air color combination for summer months. A cotton log-cabin quilt is on the bed; the one on the wall is made of pieced calico.*

IN LOVE WITH QUILTS

Phyllis Haders has been fascinated by quilts ever since she was a young girl visiting her aunt in the Indiana Amish country. A simply patterned but spectacularly colored quilt hanging on a clothesline caught her eye and "the germ was planted then," she recalls. "I had to get to know these people who were capable of creating such strange beauty."

Today, hundreds of quilts later, Phyllis Haders is a dealer in all types of American quilts and a collector of quilts and other antiques. She started by buying things she liked for her house— Canton china, spongeware, baskets—and she used her clothing allowance because these things were more important to her.

Most important to her, however, are the Amish and other American quilts, on display or carefully stored in acid-free tissue paper, available through museum supply sources and some paper companies. Contact your local museum for suppliers near you.

Iron-and-brass bed, *a turn-of-the-century piece, is covered with a "Double Irish Chain" quilt, c. 1870.*

"Drunkard's Path" quilt, *c. 1870, hangs above a small "Tumbling Home" sea chest.*

Country French armoire, *c. 1800, holds Phyllis Haders' collection of American quilts.*

103

104

A MOVING EXPERIENCE

Beverly and Tommy Jacomini found their Texas farmhouse, built in 1857 by German immigrants, when it had been abandoned as a living place and was being used to store hay. But Beverly, a partner in the Houston interior design firm of Jacomini, Holley, Tolleson, saw the potential of the house. She was especially excited by the 19th-century stenciling and the beautiful, unusually colored painted walls of the house which, although mostly obscured by the hay, were still in good condition.

To move the building to the Jacominis' property, some 25 miles away, the roof had to be removed and the house cut in half and then totally rebuilt on the new site. The Jacominis did not alter the basic structure of the house, but added electricity, plumbing, a kitchen, and a bath within the existing space. Since the house lacks closets, they use large antique armoires.

Antique quilts *in bedrooms are from Beverly Jacomini's collection. Walls are in their original blue paint.*

Pine beds *in the guest bedroom were made in Texas in the 19th century. Rag rugs and quilts are also antique.*

BED AND BATH

Designer Raymond Waites started to move away from Italian modern design when he began to collect old rustic pottery. After he bought an 18th-century Vermont pine cupboard, "my whole way of thinking shifted," he notes. "I began to believe that objects could be warmer and more comfortable, but still clean and functional."

Waites used the East Hampton, N.Y., cottage, shown here, that he bought with his wife, Nancy, as a laboratory for his design ideas. Previously associated with both Design Research stores and Marimekko, Waites credits the influences of the Scandinavian color palette and the purity and functionality of Shaker design in his work. But the products he has created for the New Country Gear collections employ a softer color palette than Scandinavian items, are warmer and more comfortable than Shaker, and show a definite American Country awareness.

Presented here is what is primarily the bath in the Waites'

Fabric-covered bed *is placed in the bathroom for relaxing or for extra guests.*

Small cupboard *is a Finnish country antique; the decoy is American.*

beach house. The space also functions as a guest bedroom, however. Since Waites believes in multifunction spaces, every room can also be used as a sleeping area.

Objects here and throughout the house are simple, rustic, clean, chosen more for their color or shape than their age or investment value. Colors in this house are all white or light colored wood, making all the rooms, including the bath, seem large and airy. And in every room, all furniture is exactly centered and symmetrical, creating the sense of complete order Waites desires.

DINING ROOMS

A separate dining room did not become a feature of American houses until the emergence of Georgian architecture in the 18th century. Until then—and even after that time in most rural areas—eating took place in the all-purpose "hall," around tables that could be taken apart, turned into seats, or made smaller by dropping the leaves, after the end of the meal. The family assembled around the table on simple stools and benches, with chairs reserved for the head of the household.

Space-saving, multipurpose tables, both antique and contemporary adaptations, are still popular today, especially for apartments and houses where dining has once again merged with the liv-

Dining table, *made of old wood, is a reproduction of one in the Metropolitan Museum. Chairs are all antique and all different.*

Redware, mochaware, *and Benningtonware stand in an 18th-century Delaware side cupboard. This dining room was originally built c. 1680.*

109

ing, cooking, and "family" spaces. Some of the tables in this section are set with antique country dinnerware—decorated redware, pewter, treenware. Most owners, however, have saved these now valuable and fragile "everyday" dishes of the past for show in their cupboards, preferring, instead, to eat on contemporary pieces with an old-fashioned country look.

CHRIS MEAD

CHRIS MEAD

TABLES FOR DINING

The earliest American tables were made of long oak boards—often six feet or more—set on thick turned legs. Over the years, a variety of table styles replaced this form, but the influence of the original Pilgrim table persisted in the rectangular harvest, sawbuck, and trestle tables most seen today.

Sawbuck tables that could be dismantled were a great space saver in the small colonial home, as were tilt-top chair-tables and, later, drop-leaf and gateleg tables.

Although the earliest tables were made of oak, later forms used a variety of woods, often combined with a pine top. The differences in woods were frequently hidden under a layer of bright-colored paint, or grain-painted (painted in a pattern to simulate wood). Tables with original paint are the most valuable.

Round table *in old pine by Rai-mundo Lemus has a tilt-top, walnut-toned stain; $750.*

Old pine *center-drawer desk by Raimundo Lemus can also be a dining table; $750.*

Drop-leaf, *19th-century table holds a stoneware crock and an old tin box.*

Chair-table *with double seat is an 18th-century New England piece. Note the drawer underneath the seat. Ladder-back armchair is from New England.*

110

Pine table *holds contemporary ce-ramic lamp and antique wooden mor-tar and pestle.*

Windsor chairs *and a 19th-century deacon's bench provide seating at an English pine dining table, c. 1820.*

Deacon's bench, *made of pine, provides seating at a pine worktable.*

Tilt-top *dining table from New England, c. 1830, becomes a seat when the round top is pushed back. Windsor chairs are also from New England.*

Rectangular table, *made of old pine by Raimundo Lemus in New York City, costs $1,200. All of Lemus's tables are custom interpretations of the Shaker style.*

CUPBOARDS

Open and corner cupboards served much the same function in the Early American house—storing china, glass, cutlery, and other household furnishings—as they do today. Almost always painted, these cupboards formed a fine background to the display of the favored dinnerware of the period and area, whether white ironstone, redware, Chinese porcelain, stoneware, or delftware.

Spongeware, *c. 1830–1840, and Canton china from the 19th century are stored in a corner cupboard.*

Red-painted, *early 19th-century pine cupboard holds antique toys, pottery, and miniature boxes.*

Welsh cupboard, *c. 1860, holds a collection of white ironstone, common dinnerware in 19th-century England and America.*

Slip-decorated *redware plates, pitcher, molds, and bowls, and stoneware fruits stand in an early 19th-century open cupboard.*

Hanging cupboard *holds English food crocks. The carved top and bottom pieces were made from Early American window valances.*

Pine cupboard, *an early 19th-century piece found in Vermont, has been intricately carved and detailed.*

American hutch, *painted red, dates to c. 1820. Inside is a collection of contemporary hand-painted plates.*

Open cupboard, *made in Ipswich, Mass., in the 17th century, displays redware and wooden-headed dolls.*

113

Black-glazed *New England redware and treenware are lined up in a red-painted step-back New England cupboard.*

Plate rack, *an American antique, hangs above an English Queen Anne settle. Rack holds a collection of antique and new pewter.*

Hearts *and swastika motifs decorate an early 19th-century English cupboard. Blue-and-white spongeware is displayed on the shelves.*

CHRIS MEAD

Ladder-back chairs *with woven seats, all primitive country pieces, were built by Appalachian people who have been making chairs in this style for generations.*

CHAIRS

Of all types of American furniture, the chair has been produced in the greatest number of forms. One of the most popular styles, made from 1700 to the present, is the ladder- or slat-back chair, named for its horizontal slats. Some of the finest examples of this style were made by the Shakers in the 19th century. Windsor chairs have also been popular over the years.

114

CHRIS MEAD

Queen Anne chair *from New Hampshire stands in a hallway.*

FRANK KOLLEOGY

Windsor chair *from New Hampshire is a "sack back," one of many types.*

J. BARRY O'ROURKE

Shaker rocker *has "mushroom caps" on the arms.*

Rustic chair, *a naïve version of the Queen Anne style, was made in Virginia in the early 20th century.*

Ladder-back chairs, *shown here on a porch at Winedale Historical Center in Round Top, Tex., were commonly made in Texas between 1840 and 1870 and were in use through the early 20th century.*

115

"Country Garden" chair, *available at the Door Store, is a contemporary ladder-back or slat-back chair.*

Rawhide seats *of the ladder-back chairs were made of calf hide that was simply stretched and dried, not treated. Tears in the seats were repaired with hide stitching. Similar chairs in the East had rush or tape seats.*

116

GEAR DESIGN

Tablecloth *in sand-colored "Country Porch" pattern and "Country Kitchen" napkin are both from the New Country Gear collection for Leacock & Co.*

J. BARRY O'ROURKE

Spongeware—*whiteware or stoneware with blue, green, or brown color applied with sponge—is reproduced by Bennington Potters, Bennington, Vt. Pieces sell for $25 to $85.*

TABLETOP IDEAS

While stoneware from Europe and even porcelain from China might have been found in the dining-room cupboard, it was the locally produced pottery—redware, yellowware, salt-glazed stoneware—that was most often used on the Early American country table.

J. BARRY O'ROURKE

Wicker basket *is a wine coaster for an al fresco luncheon (above). Decanters can be old bottles or vases, as well as fine glassware. An old wire milk bottle carrier is used here to bring small pots of plants to the table.*

Today, the once common but now valuable—and fragile—products of 18th- and 19th-century potteries stand in the display cupboard. Reproductions, both mass-produced and made by individual craftsmen, are far more practical everyday alternatives to original pieces. Contemporary adaptations—new designs with an old-fashioned feeling—can also bring a simple, rustic look to your table, as can newly made hand-painted plates from around the world. Even plain white earthenware has a farm-fresh feeling, reminiscent of 19th-century whiteware.

Important, too, in bringing the country to your table are the accessories you choose. Baskets are wonderful servers, as are rough wooden bowls and platters. Homespun cloths, or contemporary material with a homey look, can be used for napkins, place mats, and tablecloths. Flowers can be simply arranged.

Yellowware bowls, *antique baskets, and a 19th-century grain sifter serve a holiday buffet. The tablecloth is a star appliquéd quilt made in 1878.*

Pewter chargers, *or large plates, used under treenware plates, make a "layered" table setting. Reproduction pewter is made by Wilton Armetale.*

Table linens, *from New Country Gear collection for Leacock & Co., look homespun. Approximate prices are from $2.75 for napkins to $40 for tablecloths. Blue-and-white canister is graniteware—sheet iron coated with porcelainlike substance—factory-made in late 19th and early 20th centuries.*

BORROWED TIME

The interiors of Kathy and John Schoemer's 1840 Connecticut house are constantly changing. Almost everything in the house is "borrowed" from Mrs. Schoemer's business as a dealer in American country antiques, and it is all, except for a few sentimental pieces, for sale. "I enjoy a changing environment," says Kathy. "It's an advantage for me to be able to live with, at least for a while, the 18th- and 19th-century antiques I sell."

Wall cupboard, *in original red paint, holds hog-scraper candlesticks.* **Sawbuck table** *is surrounded by Canadian "salamander-back" chairs.*

118

NEW ENGLAND RE-CREATED

Although this house is furnished to resemble a New England country cottage of the last century, it is located in the Midwest. The owners, dealers in American antiques, first became interested in the field through their love of primitive paintings, and many fine examples of Early American art hang throughout the house.

Theorem painting *with stenciled frame hangs above a candle box.*

Hutch table, *unusual because of its large size, is used for dining. Bow-back Windsor side chairs and exceptionally high hoop-back armchairs are placed around the table. On the wall is a collection of New England miniature watercolors.*

CHRIS MEAD

CHRIS MEAD

BORDER LINES

Elaborate stenciling, handpainted by an itinerant artist in the mid-19th century, still decorates the combination living room/dining room of Beverly and Tommy Jacomini's Texas farmhouse. Wallboards vary in size here, the wood surface is uneven, but it all adds up to a relaxed, family atmosphere that is enhanced by the Texas antiques.

Stenciled borders *were painted about 1857. The roses were individually hand painted without a pattern.*

Texas antiques *from the mid-19th century are used for dining. Chairs have rawhide and deerskin seats.*

120

Punch-tin cupboard, *made in San Antonio, c. 1830, holds jars of tomatoes, pickles, herb vinegar, and jalapeño jelly, all preserved by Beverly Jacomini.*

DINING WITH HISTORY

Corinne Burke first entered an antiques shop to break up the boredom of a long car trip. "I walked in and saw the light!" she remembers. "I've been hooked on the objects of the past ever since." Now a dealer of American country furniture and accessories, Corinne has tried to recapture the atmosphere of the 18th and 19th centuries in her own 18th-century farmer's stone house in upstate New York. Many of her favorite

Simple crocks *were the most common form of 18th- and 19th-century stoneware.*

collections are displayed in the dining room: 18th-century pewter graces the old wooden mantel; the New England hutch table on wooden wheels is set with 18th-century treenware; and blue Canton china is displayed in the corner cupboard. Pulled up to the dining table are fanback Windsor chairs, part of a set of six made in New Hampshire. Although the artist who painted the portraits on both sides of the fireplace is unknown, Corinne has discovered that the subjects were ancestors of Daniel Webster.

Oriental rugs *were as desirable in colonial times as today. A Kazak rug covers the floor in this dining room.*

Red-painted settle, *c. 1760–1790, has been maintained in its original condition.*

122

123

SPANISH ACCENT

Alan and Shirley Minge started buying Spanish colonial home furnishings in junk shops and secondhand stores in New Mexico thirty years ago. About the same time, they began restoring Casa San Ysidro, their 18th-century Spanish New Mexican hacienda. It is the only private, historically accurate house of its type.

Dining room *includes New Mexican pine table and* trastero, *or cupboard.* **Spanish colonial** *pine bench, originally painted blue, is c. 1800.*

Wooden shelves *hold European ceramics that would have been displayed in a Spanish New Mexican house after the Santa Fe Trail opened.*

KITCHENS

The keeping room, a descendant of the medieval "hall," was America's first kitchen. This was the main (and often, only) room in the house, and its fireplace was both the architectural and domestic focal point of the building. Here the family gathered to cook, get warm, and do their indoor chores by firelight.

When houses expanded with the increased wealth of the Georgian period (or later in frontier areas), the colonists separated the kitchen from the rest of the house. In New England it was often an ell at the back of the building, an effort to isolate the heat and cooking odors. In the warm South it was sometimes a separate out-building, a strictly functional space.

Today many homeowners have re-created the warmth of the old colonial kitchens, making it more of a family and entertainment area than a purely utilitarian space.

Some have atmospheric old stoves and original old cabinets and woodwork. But even those kitchens filled with modern appliances and conveniences can have a country mood, created by the baskets, and other accessories.

127

Barn kitchen *combines old beams with energy-efficient appliances (left).* **Kitchen utensils** *from the 17th to 19th centuries surround the hearth of this 17th-century house (right).*

FRANK KOLLEOGY

Back porch, *located off the dining room of this Virginia house, is used to serve buffets and to store crocks, baskets, molds, and outdoor cooking tools.*

128

Scraps of tin, *left over from making other utensils or saved from old canisters, were frequently made into cookie cutters by itinerant craftsmen.*

KITCHEN UTENSILS

Through the 17th, 18th, and most of the 19th centuries, factory-processed foodstuffs were not available. Nearly all food had to be prepared at home by the housewife. It is not surprising, therefore, that countless utensils—including some whose functions are a mystery to us today— were developed to ease the kitchen workload. Apple corers,

Iron utensils *were made in Mexico and New Mexico of iron shipped from Mexico City. These 100-to-200-year-old pieces are very rare today.*

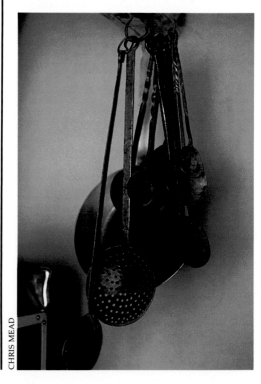

nutmeg grinders, sugar cutters, as well as forks, pots, and spatulas, were devised in many forms.

Most valued today are the handmade objects in wood and metal that were used from the 17th to 19th centuries in preparing meals at the open hearth. Less valuable, but also eagerly collected, are the machine-made utensils used on the wood and coal ranges that were first sold in the mid-19th century. The implements that are easiest to find are those that have undergone few design changes over the years.

Spatterware pot *by General Housewares Corp. is reminiscent of old farmhouse utensils. "Cook's Cloth" underneath is from Barth & Dreyfuss.*

Country kitchen *implements include antique tin candle mold, measure, funnel, and a basket, c. 1850, made to hold keys.*
Wood beam *is used to hold wire and natural fiber baskets (left).*
Galvanized pipe, *attached to a beam, is a good way to store cooking utensils within easy reach.*

129

STOVES

Woodburning stoves are making a comeback. Franklin, parlor, and other cast-iron devices, outmoded by central heating in the late 19th century, are once again popular as alternative energy sources, as well as for their charm. Antique cooking stoves also provide old-time atmosphere, though most cooks today prefer modern stoves for primary cooking chores. Reproductions are now manufactured by a number of firms.

130

Sleek kitchen, *a contrast to the rest of this 1825 farmhouse, includes a Corning ceramic-cook-top stove.*

Wall ovens *by Caloric (above) were chosen for this converted barn's kitchen because of their energy efficiency. This room blends old beams and accessories with white tile and modern appliances.*

Cast-iron stove *(below), still in use in a restored New Mexico hacienda, was originally transported by railroad from Colorado at the turn of the century. Old copper utensils on the stove are from Mexico.*

Woodburning stove, *manufactured by Russo, stands on a platform to make loading easier.*

Victorian-era Franklin stove *warms the den of this converted, late-19th-century carriage house.*

"Home Comfort" woodburning stove, *manufactured c. 1924, is still in use in the house of artist Tommy Simpson. Made of cast iron with blue graniteware enameling, the stove is also decorated with whimsical socks handmade and painted by Simpson. The graniteware pots on the stove are late 19th century. The large copper pitcher on the floor is an English milk container, also late 19th century.*

131

Industrial-style lighting—*inexpensive and readily available—is attached to the old beams added to the new space. Lamps can be angled to spotlight any task. Woven and wire baskets hang from hooks on the beams; other baskets rest on top.*

132

Small kitchen *is a completely new space added onto the house. The room is tiny, but efficient; all utensils are within view and easy to find. Countertops are made of tongue-and-groove wood flooring. Floors, walls, and appliances are white.*

ROBERT GRANT/GEAR DESIGN

OPEN TO VIEW

Everything needed for cooking is visible in the kitchen of designer Raymond Waites and his wife, Nancy. Whether hanging from the beams, standing in open shelves, or hooked onto the pegboards, these functional items are an essential part of the decor.

Pegboard wall *holds baskets and pine dish and cutlery racks by Sunglow. Animal-shaped pitchers stand on the racks on top.*

133

CHRIS MEAD

Window shade *is made of contemporary fabric, attached to a roller.*

134

KITCHEN EXPANSION

Corinne Burke's kitchen is now twice the size it was when the house was built in 1776. Using old beams and boards for walls and ceilings and bricks from a dismantled chimney for the floor, she created space to work and space to dine, separated by a half wall and the old settle.

Settle bed, *19th-century version of the "convertible couch," was a closed bench during the day, a bed at night.*

Miniature carvings *and old kitchen utensils are displayed on a shelf.*

Homemade preserves *are stored over the Revolutionary-era door.*

Plate rack, *a New England antique, let dishes drip over a dry sink. Today it still hangs above a dry sink, but stores dinnerware straight from the dishwasher.*

THE HEART OF OUR HOME

This is the Emmerling kitchen, where our family really lives. It is a very large space that we remodeled with modern equipment, yet it is warm and homey too. The old woods and soft, aged colors of the primitive furnishings—the pine hutch and table, the painted chairs, the drying racks—seem to add a character and friendliness all their own.

I particularly like the combination of country warmth with up-to-date convenience in this room: industrial lamps provide light over the old table and the easy-to-clean white tile floor is a wonderful background for the textures of wood, baskets, and plants.

We use everything here—nothing is simply for decoration. I serve on the pewter plates and stoneware bowls in the hutch; the standing rack dries the herbs I grow in the window, and the rack on the wall is for cooling cookies.

Functional kitchen, *organized around pine harvest table, combines modern white appliances with furniture of old wood. An especially handy device is the ironing board that opens out of the closet.*

CHRIS MEAD

Sweet-smelling *herbs, and sometimes geraniums, grow in a box by the window—we are fortunate to have an unusual amount of sun for a city apartment. I dry the herbs by hanging them upside down on a rack nearby, and there are always plenty of baskets around for displaying plants.*

A CHANGE OF TASTE

When the owners of this renovated, mid-19th-century potting shed first started collecting antiques, they were interested in Victorian pieces. In time, their tastes changed, and they discovered that they preferred the older, more primitive style of furnishings. Since they also enjoy modern convenience, they employed interior designer John Saladino to help them update their house, combining the comfort and practicality of today with furniture and accessories from their collection of primitives.

The kitchen, situated in the oldest part of the house (a new wing was added twenty years ago), was four rooms when the house was first built as the potting shed of a large Connecticut estate. Over the years, it became three rooms, then two, and now Saladino has opened the space en-

tirely, turning it into one large, light-filled kitchen-dining room combination. The Formica-topped, knotty-pine counters designed by Saladino—new and practical, but with a rustic feeling—separate the two areas. New, too, but definitely in the country mood, is the pine dining table, also designed by Saladino. When this space became one room, the old crossbeams in the ceiling were revealed and stripped to the original wood. Now "it's the best part of the kitchen."

The owners also enjoy the fact that although the room is white and sky lit, it is not sterile, but is warmed by the natural wood tones and their antiques.

Open shelves (left) are used for storage in the kitchen. Pine counters and table were designed by John Saladino.
Stoneware crocks (right) from New York and Vermont and a 19th-century cast-iron horse and carriage sit above a passageway. Chair is Victorian.

FRANK KOLLEOGY

SOUTHERN COMFORT

Muskettoe Pointe Farm, the Tidewater, Va., area home of Pat and Jim Carter, was an overgrown ruin when they bought it. The small 17th-century house was "leaning at a funny angle," and there was little remaining of the gardens that once surrounded it. But an architect-friend from Colonial Williamsburg confirmed that the 1680 structure was sound, and the Carters, along with their nine children and the help of local carpenters and masons, set about restoring and enlarging the house and planting formal and herb gardens.

They first added a kitchen (the original house had only a tacked-on 19th-century kitchen) and laundry, with bedrooms and bath above. They later turned that kitchen into the dining room and added the room shown here. To make an "invisible" transition between the two parts, they cut into the floor planks of the dining room and interlocked the boards with planks in the new wing.

Today, the kitchen is a blend of modern convenience and country comfort; up-to-date appliances and antique furnishings from both Europe and the surrounding Virginia countryside. To maintain an authentic colonial look, the kitchen cabinets were ingeniously formed by using the facing from old corner cupboards.

Almost all the family's entertaining starts here, with meals served buffet-style on the tables and on boards placed over the sink. Kept burning all winter, the fire adds to the warmth and charm that makes this kitchen the family's favorite gathering place.

Drying herbs *hang by the fire on a rack made of grapevines. Antique English bench, table, and chair stand underneath.*

Virginia settle, *made of maple, is placed next to the dining table, an 18th-century French baker's table.*

CHRIS MEAD

140

SPANISH AMERICAN

The Spanish-style exterior of this adobe brick house is in keeping with its Arizona neighbors. Inside, however, the mood is pure Americana, with all rooms planned to display the owners' extensive collection of antiques.

Iron pig *is a butcher's shop sign, c. 1850. Antique salesmen's samples, toys, and miniature utensils hang above the stove.*

Showcase, *made in the 1850s as a tabletop display, has been turned upright to hold miniature baskets.*

142

CHRIS MEAD

CHRIS MEAD

GARDEN VARIETY

More than 200 varieties of herbs and vegetables grow in Barbara and Mel Ohrbach's country garden. And these are an integral part of the decoration of their house, whether drying on old racks, arranged in bowls, or used as potpourri, filling the whole house with lovely scents.

Appliqué quilt, *made in New Hampshire in the 19th century, hangs behind a 19th-century French table.*

Homespun cloths, *both American and French, are napkins and towels.*

143

FARMHOUSE KITCHEN

When something old appeals to Houston interior designer Beverly Jacomini, she doesn't spare any work to make it live up to its potential. The turn-of-the-century stove below was "nothing but rust" when Beverly brought it home. She cleaned it, had it electrified, and now the stove stands, surrounded by Texas antiques, old-fashioned spatterware, and old canisters and signs, in the center of the farmhouse kitchen.

Pie safe *(right), with screened front and sides, was made in Texas.*

Handmade cupboard *(below) has drawers lined with tin for use as canisters and a shelf that pulls out.*

144

CHRIS MEAD

CHRIS MEAD

CHRIS MEAD

P · A · R · T · III

COUNTRY ELEMENTS

149

It is the simple country elements—a basketful of fresh flowers, a knife box set on a table, a window box planted with fresh herbs—that help introduce a country theme to a contemporary residence and provide the finishing touches to a traditional country house. To acquaint you with the possibilities, this section presents a full array of country accessories, from quilts to bottles to baskets, that can produce a country look in virtually every room in the house—and on porches, patios, and terraces—with little cost or effort. And since nothing makes you feel more a part of the country than growing your own plants, included here are traditional flower, vegetable, and herb gardens, and suggestions for plantings on terraces and throughout the house.

CHRIS MEAD

BASKETS, QUILTS, AND OTHER IMPORTANT ACCESSORIES

Country accessories such as breadboards, baskets, and knife boxes were in daily use in the past and can be put to good use again today. Some items—antique quilts and coverlets, breakable bottles and pottery—may be too valuable and fragile for hard, everyday wear and tear, but their display in the home helps to create an informal, country mood.

Portraits, theorem paintings, memorial paintings, and landscapes of the 18th and 19th centuries are the most authentic types of artwork for your home. Unfortunately, current prices put these paintings, as well as the work of the better known contemporary

Antique tools *on the wall, hooked rug, quilt, and baskets are important accessories in this 19th-century Nantucket house. Table and Windsor chairs are 18th century.*

Rocking horse, *a turn-of-the-century child's toy, is now an accessory.*

folk artists, far beyond the reach of most people. Consider, instead, displaying humbler items on your walls as art: checkerboards, needlework, hooked rugs. Boldly patterned and colored quilts make an immediate statement, whether hung on the wall or covering a bed, and are a

highly regarded art form. Their prices, however, are still below those of most paintings.

Don't hesitate to put your accessories to new uses. Knife and tool boxes, for example, can certainly hold cutlery and screwdrivers, but they are also practical organizers for stationery supplies and other odds and ends.

Your accessories do not have to be old and handmade to have a country flavor. Good reproductions of early pottery and newly made quilts and baskets can bring much the same feeling to your home as antiques, and have the advantage of being less expensive and more readily available.

And consider, too, the work of craftsmen who still do things in the exacting, time-honored way. Because they are handmade, much of the pottery, baskets, glassware, and textiles made today have the look of the past.

151

Country baskets *lined with foil make perfect containers for plants.*

Fireplace logs *can be stored on the hearth in large, laundry-style basket.*

Oversized drying basket *on a white wall adds warmth.*

A BOUNTY OF BASKETS

There are never too many baskets in the country house. You will find a purpose for every shape and size, from the smallest trinket case to the largest clothes basket. But don't hide your collection—display your baskets for simple decoration.

Baskets displayed are baskets you will remember to use. At far left, antique field and produce baskets hang from a curtain rod; miniature baskets are on the ledge for show.

Indian baskets *placed atop an old painted cupboard provide storage.*

Splint basket, *a common hand-crafted shape, was carried to market.*

153

Farm baskets, *originally used for carrying produce from the field and then to market, hang from the rafters of a New England kitchen.*

COMFORTING QUILTS

The earliest American quilts were made of solid pieces of cloth fastened together with elaborate stitching. The pieced and appliquéd quilts that are most common today developed in the late 18th century. In general, the earlier the quilt, the finer the stitching. Later examples are frequently prized for their color and pattern.

154

"Lone Star" *crib quilt, used as a wall hanging, was made in New York State in the late 19th century.*

"Stuffed work" quilt *was made in Pennsylvania, c. 1860, by adding bits of cotton underneath the appliquéd design until it was fully padded.*

Patchwork coasters *are made of plexiglass-encased quilt squares.*

Pillows *in patchwork patterns were made from old quilt pieces.*

"Birds in Air" quilt, *c. 1875, is used instead of a headboard in this bedroom. An "Eight-Pointed Star" quilt, c. 1877, covers the bed.*

155

Crib quilt, *the perfect size for a small space, is appliquéd in a floral pattern.*

"Star of Bethlehem," a contemporary quilt, *covers a modern platform bed. A portrait, c. 1840, of the Prior-Hamblen school hangs over the blanket chest.*

A SLICE OF LIFE

Watermelons bring to mind country picnics on the Fourth of July. In the past, a watermelon was often the center of a still-life theorem painting. Today it is a favorite motif of a number of contemporary folk artists. Miles Carpenter of Waverly, Va., first carved a watermelon slice as a trade sign for his ice business. Now, slices by Carpenter may cost as much as $1,000 each. New Mexico artist Felipe Archuleta made his first watermelon at the suggestion of a friend, folk art dealer Davis Mather. A whole watermelon with a slice removed is now a motif associated with Archuleta.

Watermelons, *in profusion (opposite), are an appealing sight.*

Folk artist *Felipe Archuleta carves watermelons in many sizes.*

Hooked rug, *a multicolored still life, was made in California.*

Red-and-green *Virginia cupboard holds Miles Carpenter's watermelons.*

Mounted slice *with knife for eating was carved by Miles Carpenter.*

157

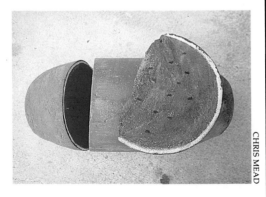

Unusual watermelon *by Felipe Archuleta has a cutout wedge.*

Full-size watermelon *was hand carved by artist Felipe Archuleta.*

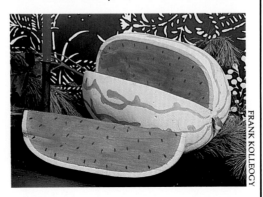

Primitive watermelon *was recently made by an amateur artist as a gift.*

WALL DISPLAYS

The Early Americans frequently displayed their best possessions—pewter, silver, china—on wall shelves hanging in the main halls (living rooms) of their houses. And since storage space was at a premium in these small cottages, they often hung household utensils directly on the wall as well.

Today, hanging shelves are still a good way to display small collectibles that might be lost in larger cupboards or in large rooms.

158

New England *hanging shelf holds antique books, church carvings, and miniatures.*

Many collectibles *combine to form this successful kitchen arrangement: a hooked rug, c. 1920, reproduction quilting patterns, antique baskets, cookie cutters, molds, and boards.*

Storage shelf, *once used in a barn to store nails, is a showcase for miniature folk art objects.*

Miniature bandboxes, *covered with wallpaper, once held small trinkets.*

Candle box, *a 19th-century Connecticut piece painted red, now holds small collectibles as well as candles.*

Hanging shelf, *c. 1830, displays pillows made from quilts.*

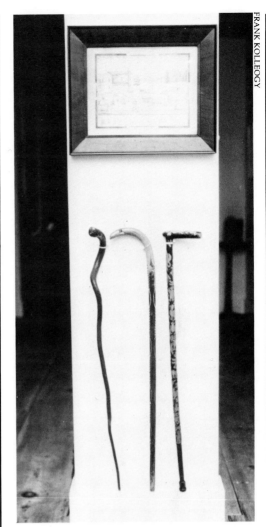

159

Antique canes *and a folk art drawing from Pennsylvania decorate a narrow wall.*

However, you don't have to use shelves made for this purpose to show off your objects. A nail or tool box, hung on its side, or an old printer's type box also make excellent display cases.

It is convenient and attractive to hang the collectibles you use on the wall. Plan your arrangement by laying the objects out on the floor before hanging them.

WOODEN BOXES

The Early American home was filled with a wide variety of boxes for holding all sorts of household goods: cutlery, spices, candles, books, documents, and other personal belongings. And the tool shed and barn had almost as many types—tool carriers of all sizes and grain sorters, for example. Many of these wooden boxes were decorated, either by carving or with bright painted designs.

160

Country toolbox, *a primitive piece, holds cutlery for a party buffet. This type of box can be used throughout the house—depending on size and shape, it can hold stationery, books, children's toys, nuts and candy during the holidays.*

Books *are toted in a toolbox.*

Grain box *now sorts stationery.*

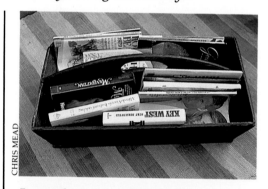

Large box *now holds books.*

Small toys *are organized in an old tool or nail box, painted red.*

Toolbox *is large enough to efficiently organize desk-top paraphernalia.*

Knife box *carries children's play-things from one room to another.*

Photo credit (vertical): J. BARRY O'ROURKE

Wood candlestands, *made in New England in the 17th and 18th centuries, are adjustable so the flame can be raised as the candle burns down, and the light moved according to the task at hand. Some also have swing arms.*

CANDLE POWER

While today we rely on candles mainly for atmosphere, they were precious commodities to the Early American housewife, who made her candles of tallow, beeswax, or bayberry, and stored them, along with stubs, in boxes designed to keep out rodents. The most common form of candle holder in 19th-century rural America was the hog scraper candlestick, named for its resemblance to a tool used for taking bristles off hides.

Photo credit (vertical): CHRIS MEAD

Jack-o'-lantern *was crafted of tin and painted in New York, c. 1875.*

Photo credit (vertical): CHRIS MEAD

Hog scraper *candlesticks.*

Photo credit (vertical): GEAR DESIGN/ROBERT GRANT

An array *of candles adds atmosphere.*

Photo credit (vertical): CHRIS MEAD

Candy molds *used as candle holders.*

Photo credit (vertical): GEAR DESIGN/ROBERT GRANT

Candle holders *are contemporary.*

PLANTS, FLOWERS, AND GARDENS

The garden is a natural extension of the country house. The view outside the windows, constantly changing with the seasons, is an integral part of the decoration, and few who own a bit of earth can resist the temptation to dirty their hands by planting herbs, vegetables, and flowers.

The garden yields a bounty for the senses—fresh vegetables, herbs, and fruits for cooking, drying, and preserving, and fresh-cut flowers for bowls and vases.

Even if you live in the city, you can still enjoy the relaxation and rewards of gardening. With a terrace, the possibilities are endless—trees, shrubs, vegetables,

Herbs, vegetables, *and flowers dry suspended from lines attached to the ceiling of a country store. When fully dried, they can be stored and used for cooking and decoration.*

flowers, can flourish with the proper care. A sunny window box will grow more than enough herbs for your kitchen. And indoor plants create a country atmosphere all by themselves.

Devoted gardener *Virginia Sal-*

adino starts most of her vegetables from seed, often well before recommended dates, believing that "you have little to lose and may gain some valuable time." She uses no pesticides, only a spray made from blended garlic, hot peppers, and water.

163

Culinary herbs *are the core of any herb garden. Chives, parsley, dill, basil, rosemary, and mint are the beginner's basics. Dry what you cannot use fresh.*

HERB GARDENS

Herb gardens were an absolute necessity to the colonial home. In addition to growing herbs for curing and flavoring foods, Early American housewives also raised herbs for many of the things we now buy in stores: insect repellents, cosmetics, dyes, medicines. Today, you can grow herbs anywhere there is sunshine and soil that is not overly rich. Apartment dwellers can easily grow herbs indoors in pots.

Herbs in pots *can be brought indoors for their fragrance and use in the kitchen. When tending herbs indoors, select a well-lit space with cool air.*

Growing plants *to start an herb garden can be bought at nurseries.*

CHRIS MEAD

Herb gardens *in Early American times were located near the house, either by the kitchen or the front door.*

Rosemary

There's Rosemary,
that's for
remembrance;
pray you love,
remember.

CHRIS MEAD

Rosemary, *the symbol of fidelity, is an age-old cure for loss of memory.*

FRANK KOLLEOGY

165

Wide paths *for easy access and neat compact borders are herb garden necessities. For good looks, gardens should be weedless, with the same plants repeated often.*

Milk carriers *from the past make toting plants from garden to kitchen an easy task.*

J. BARRY O'ROURKE

Straight rows *with space between for easy access, offer a convenient way to grow certain types of vegetables. Planted here are eggplant, bush beans, kale, carrots, and celery.*

VEGETABLE GARDENS

Growing their own vegetables was a fact of life for the self-sufficient rural Early Americans. Today, too, many people find it necessary to raise their own vegetables in order to obtain produce of high quality. And you can make sure that you have the ripest vegetables when you pick them from your own backyard.

You can grow most vegetables anywhere the soil is well drained and there is plenty of sunlight. A

Lettuce *and beans are among the easiest vegetables to grow.*

Fresh herbs *(above) and salad vegetables—lettuce, tomatoes, cucumbers, and onions—are a fine combination for a small kitchen garden or for stepped terraces.*

plot 24 by 24 feet will grow more than enough vegetables for four people, but even a garden as small as 50 square feet will provide abundant salad ingredients for your table. You can even grow vegetables—especially the dwarf varieties—on city terraces.

Plan your garden on paper before you plant. Grow only as much as you can use, and rotate your crops to keep your yield high. To determine planting times for your part of the country, check with the local U.S. Weather Service branch for the average date of the last killing frost. Then follow directions on seed packages.

Many country gardeners, aware of the harsh effects of chemicals

Early Americans *believed in starting and ending a meal with lettuce.*

on the environment, have returned to the practices of the past, using "organic" fertilizers and sprays made from garlic or soap and water to repel pests. "Companion planting" of insect-deterring flowers among the vegetables is also recommended.

Lettuce leaves *should be picked from the heads as needed and used soon after picking to prevent wilting. Head lettuce varieties, shown here, can be grown in shady spots.*

167

"Companion planting" *is a natural form of insect control. Here zinnias are the "trap plants," used to distract insects from the vegetables.*

FLOWER GARDENS

If properly planned to combine flowering shrubs, spring bulbs, and hardy perennials, your garden will be blooming from the first warm day well into the winter. Garden expert Elvin McDonald recommends, however, that you keep your plan simple, growing masses of a few types of plants rather than a wide variety. When laying out your garden, make sure that the flowers will be seen to best advantage from inside the house, as well as outside.

168

Pink peonies *are hardy perennials that can be planted one fall and left to flower for years. Perennials make beautiful borders. Plant a few types that bloom in different months for constant color.*

Neat borders *of white and rose peonies, red Oriental poppies, early yellow day lilies, and lavender blue German iris are evidence of a well-planned garden. If you want to grow flowers specifically for cutting, choose a well-drained plot that receives at least a half day of sun. Plant the flowers in rows as you would vegetables, and cut, using sharp shears, in the early evening or morning when the blooms are at peak condition but before they are full blown. Place in water.*

Undraped windows *are covered only by a natural curtain of Jerusalem artichoke flowers. Here, plants growing outside are part of indoor decoration.*

Cacti and succulents, *native American plants, are mostly found in sunny, hot, dry regions, although they can also be grown in colder climates where the soil is well drained. Desert gardens need great care, and special preparation is necessary to overcome the arid conditions. Requirements include windbreaks, to protect against hot, drying winds, an irrigation system, and soil improved with humus.*

Hollyhocks, *popular in colonial gardens, grow well along fences where there is support for their height.*

Brick terrace *is decorated with twig furniture and surrounded by flowering plants and potted shrubs.*

Flower-filled *boxes can be moved around the garden to provide color. Pots, tubs, and baskets are also good for container gardening. Remember to water often.*

Palisade fence *at Colonial Williamsburg is formed of double sawtooth boards. The many fence designs here range from rough barriers to Chippendale patterns.*

Horizontal rail *fence surrounds a field in Appalachia. In the past, fields were fenced to keep the animals out; today, we fence in the animals instead.*

FENCES

Fences were originally built to protect the home and fields against enemies, wild and domestic animals, and bad weather. Simple wooden fences were common where timber was plentiful, and some Early American picket fences were hand carved by craftsmen in interesting shapes. Today these designs can be reproduced. You can also use old railroad ties or uncarved logs.

Split rails *are used here to make a primitive version of a woven fence.*

Plants grow *through open spaces in the fence logs.*

CHRIS MEAD

Spade-shaped *finials decorate a red-painted fence and gate.*

CHRIS MEAD

"Pailing fence" *is pointed to keep chickens from perching.*

CHRIS MEAD

Palisade fence *built of unfinished logs provides a rustic background for flowering plants. This type of fence can be easily and inexpensively constructed.*

171

CHRIS MEAD

Untrimmed logs *form a palisade fence in the middle of the New Mexico countryside. In many areas of the West, wood can be gathered free (with a permit) in the national forests—an inexpensive way to find fencing.*

FLOWERS IN THE HOUSE

Flowers have been popular decorations in the American home since the 18th century. While ornamental flower holders and carefully arranged bouquets were common in city parlors, in the country people made do with stoneware and baskets.

Their informal, unconstructed displays of flowers and greenery are still most suited to the country house. For containers, look

Wooden flat, *holding forced white tulips, repeat this room's color combination of rustic wood against a white background. Whole flats of plants, available at nurseries and some florists, can also be replanted after the original blooms die.*

172

White flowers—*hyacinth, lilac, ranunculus, and paper-white narcissus—can have an informal look when arranged in simple pitchers.*

Stoneware pitcher *holds a bouquet of daffodils and narcissus. These harbingers of spring, along with tulips, can be grown from bulbs in your garden and the bulbs saved for reuse. A lovely spring arrangement combines these plants with flowering branches: forsythia, quince, cherry, almond, or apple.*

Wooden wagon, *once a child's toy, is also an ingenious plant stand. Colorful country flower arrangement by New York City's Mädderlake florists includes ranunculus, sparaxis, and snapdragons. The wooden bowl holds potpourri.*

around the house to see what you can use. Baskets with any type of waterproof liner are perfect. William Jarecki of New York City's Mädderlake florists also recommends stoneware crocks, Shaker boxes, redware, and old terra-cotta, but not new clay pots—they are too bright in color and look machine-made. Old buckets, handcrafted pottery, and wooden flats from the local nursery are also suitable.

Naturally, the plants you use depend on the season, and remember that you do not need many plants to bring the outdoors in. A single flower at a place setting or a lone sprig of greenery in a crock is also effective.

Simple planters *and containers are best for showing off flowers in and around the country house. A half-round copper planter from Mexico (above left), hanging on an outside wall, holds a flowering browallia. Inside, a wicker basket displays purple and white hydrangea blossoms (above right).*

Daffodil *and narcissus need no elaborate arranging.*
One flower *at every place is an alternative to centerpieces.*

FRANK KOLLEOGY

Overgrown ivy *and mossy bricks outline a city garden too shady to support most flowering plants. The space is multileveled to make optimum use of a small area. Some plants are potted so they can be easily moved.*

174

CHRIS MEAD

Twig furniture, *newly made of willow by Christopher Design in Dallas, Tex. suits the rustic mood of this restored 1857 central Texas farmhouse porch.*

PORCHES AND TERRACES

In the days before air conditioning, the porch was summer's living room. Shaded from the sun and cooled by plants and passing breezes, the porch is still an enjoyable, energy-efficient spot to spend warm days.

There are many hardy varieties of herbs, flowers, and vegetables that can survive the less than optimum growing conditions of city gardens and terraces. Urban plants need enriched soil, light, and, especially, sufficient water.

FRANK KOLLEOGY

Antique wicker *brings a country mood to an ivy-and-brick city garden.*

Lilac-covered *terrace is in the restored Moravian community of Old Salem, N.C.*

Screened porch *is furnished with Lancaster County, Pa., antiques.*
Sapling logs *are natural supports for unstructured screening (right).*

175

SLEEPING PORCH

Cedar barn doors on two sides open Raymond and Nancy Waites' porch to the beach beyond. Used for sleeping in the summer, the room was not insulated in an effort to maintain the rustic quality of the walls and the look of sunlight streaming through the open spaces in the slats.

Beach chairs, *covered with fabric, are stored on the cedar-slat walls. Old rack is used for drying flowers.*

Barn doors *can be opened on the bottom, top, or both. Doors are made of cedar to prevent decay.*

Wicker sofas *become beds when the porch is used for sleeping. Simple wooden beach chairs can be used for extra seating when entertaining.*

THE GREAT OUTDOORS

While Beverly and Tommy Jacomini's city house is decorated in a contemporary style, they have made this house, an 1857 farmhouse in the Texas countryside, a rustic and casual retreat for family and friends. Here they entertain informally, often on the front porch they enlarged to its present grand size and filled with antique and new twig furniture. Guests help pick fresh produce from the

Twig furniture, *newly made of willow, is manufactured by Christopher Design in Dallas, Tex.*

Footstool *made of twigs is covered with an antique quilt piece.*

garden, join in the cooking, then gather on the porch, cooled by passing breezes and old-fashioned ceiling fans, to watch the moon reflected on the pond. "Our most memorable times are spent right here," says Beverly.

Farmhouse *was built in the mid-19th century by German immigrants to Texas and moved 25 miles.*

179

IV

CHRIS MEAD

FRANK KOLLEOGY

P   A   R   T   IV

COUNTRY LIVING

183

Firelit rooms, home-baked foods, holidays celebrated with friends and family—all contribute to the special quality of life in the country. To help bring the taste of the country to your home, this section includes recipes for the simple, hearty fare enjoyed by generations of Americans.

Presented in this section too are examples of how urban and rural families celebrate a country Christmas, with holiday vignettes created with inexpensive, easily put-together decorations. Included as well are instructions for making a charming wreath and recipes for festive foods to give as gifts.

CHRIS MEAD

AMERICAN COUNTRY FOOD

Country foods are simple, wholesome, and fresh. They are foods that are chosen with care, easy to prepare, and eaten with a hearty appetite. At best, they are foods acquired close to their source, whether picked from your garden, fished from the sea, or bought at local roadside stands. In summer, especially, country cooks can take advantage of the natural bounty of land and sea, and those whose skills include pickling and preserving can enjoy the fruits of the summer all year long.

Don't be afraid to experiment with your fresh-picked herbs and produce. And don't be afraid to substitute for missing ingredients. Remember our original country

Fruit jars, *with 19th-century design, are still available today from Ball Corp., Muncie, Ind., and Kerr Glass, Sand Springs, Okla.*

The best produce *(next to homegrown), preserves, and local specialties are found at roadside stands. This stall serves the Amish of Pennsylvania.*

cooks, who frequently had to improvise, developed the recipes we cherish today.

We call these foods American, partly, perhaps, to emphasize the ease with which they can be cooked for weekend guests or packed for a picnic. But in truth, like this nation itself, American country food is a blending of ethnic traditions, a mixture of the heritages we bring to our cooking.

The recipes that follow were collected from old friends and new acquaintances, the people who contributed their houses and thoughts to this book. They are all foods we love and want to share.

185

EASY RECIPES WITH GARDEN-FRESH HERBS AND VEGETABLES

Herb butter, pictured here in a container made of scooped-out fresh cabbage, is particularly delicious on freshly baked bread. If the herbs are chopped in a food processor, the butter becomes a brighter green. Herb butter may be stored 1 week in the refrigerator or frozen indefinitely.

Add 1 small bunch parsley, chopped, and 1 small bunch dill, chopped, to 1 pound sweet butter at room temperature. Beat until butter is fluffy and herbs are well distributed. Pack in jar and seal.

Dried herbs can also be used for herb butter. This recipe was provided by Pat Carter.

Combine 2 tablespoons each of dried, crushed thyme, basil, tarragon, and chervil with ½ cup dry white wine in a small bowl. Let set for 2 or more hours. Beat ½ cup butter until soft; add herb mixture to taste. Pack in small jar and seal.

Fresh vegetables are best eaten as soon after they are picked as possible. Since this is not always practical, here are some hints for storing vegetables.

Store the vegetables dry—don't wash them until you are ready to use them.

Except for tomatoes, vegetables should be kept cold. Keep corn on ice and don't shuck until you are ready to cook it. Peas should not be shelled until you are ready to use them or, if necessary, should only be refrigerated shelled for a few hours.

Store vegetables in a plastic bag unless you plan to use them within a few hours. This prevents moisture

from escaping.

Keep tomatoes at room temperature, away from the sun and the heat of the stove. They should be stored in one layer, preferably in a container that lets the air circulate around them.

Vegetables will retain their bright color if they are boiled for a few minutes, then rinsed in ice water before cooking is resumed.

KAREN RADKAI/HOUSE & GARDEN

The favorite dip *in the Emmerling house is made with softened cream cheese, milk, chives, paprika, and chopped onions, all to taste.*

Herb dip *pictured here is made with ¾ cup mayonnaise, ¾ cup sour cream, ⅓ cup parsley, 3 tablespoons chives, 1 crushed clove of garlic, 1 tablespoon vinegar, ⅛ teaspoon salt, and ¼ teaspoon pepper. Combine all ingredients and refrigerate overnight. Makes 1½ cups.*

A simple dip *combines 1 cup sour cream (or half sour cream, half mayonnaise) with fresh herbs, such as parsley, chives, and dill (½ to 1 tablespoon of each). Also add dash of salt, pepper, minced garlic, or chopped scallions to taste.*

187

Roast chicken and fresh vegetables of the season are an ideal combination.

Preheat oven to 425°.

Rinse and dry two 3-pound chickens. Sprinkle each, inside and out, with coarse Kosher salt. Cut 2 cloves of garlic in half, rub the chickens all over with the cut garlic, and place the garlic halves inside the chicken. Squeeze the juice of 2 lemons inside and outside the chickens, then tie the chickens with string, and place in a roasting pan.

Sprinkle chickens with freshly ground black pepper, and place in oven for 1 hour. Do not open the oven.

Remove the string and place chickens on a serving platter. Garnish with watercress or julienned vegetables.

Drain the juices into a measuring cup, skim off fat, and pour into a gravy boat. Serves about six.

Raw and quick-cooked vegetables make delicious, low-calorie hors d'oeuvres. Serve with your favorite dip.

Blanch for 1 to 2 minutes in boiling water: snow peas, carrot sticks, thin asparagus, broccoli, cauliflower, zucchini. Drain, rinse with ice water, and refrigerate until ready to use. Serve uncooked: mushrooms, red and green pepper strips, cucumber slices, scallions.

HOMEMADE SPECIALTIES FROM THE KITCHENS OF AMERICA

Glazed Virginia Country Ham is a crowd-pleasing recipe (with lots of leftovers) developed by Martha Stewart.

Soak a 12 to 16-pound ham for 10 to 12 hours in cold water to cover. Rinse ham and scrub rind thoroughly.

Place ham, skin side down, in a large pot (a large fish poacher will work). Cover with cold water. Bring to the boil and simmer 20 minutes per pound of ham.

Remove ham from the water. Using a sharp knife, remove the tough outer skin, leaving a layer of fat around the ham. Score the surface of the ham with the knife to make a decorative pattern.

Preheat the oven to 350°.

Mix 1 pound dark brown sugar and ½ cup dry sherry to form a thick sauce. Spoon the sauce over the ham and bake for two hours, or until the glaze is golden and crisp. Serve warm or at room temperature.

Corn bread, whether baked in a 9-by-9-inch square pan, in a muffin tin, or an old-fashioned stick pan, as shown here, gives a real down-home feeling to a meal.
Preheat oven to 425°.

Assemble ¾ cup all-purpose flour, 2½ teaspoons double-acting baking powder, 1 to 2 tablespoons sugar (according to taste), ¾ teaspoon salt, 1¼ cups stone-ground white or yellow cornmeal, 1 egg, 2 to 3 tablespoons melted butter or drippings, and 1 cup milk.

Grease the pan with butter, oil, or bacon drippings and place in the oven until sizzling hot. Sift together flour, baking powder, sugar, and salt. Add cornmeal.

In a separate bowl beat egg, then add melted butter or drippings, and milk, and beat together.

Combine all ingredients. Place the batter in the hot pan. Bake sticks

about 15 minutes. If you are making corn bread or muffins, cook 20 to 25 minutes. You will have 15 2-inch muffins. Serve hot.

Herb vinegar can be made with many different kinds of herbs—basil, French tarragon, chives, garlic, or sweet marjoram. Each one has its own distinctive bouquet and each will make a salad taste totally different. The following method for making vinegar from any of these herbs was provided by Barbara Ohrbach.

Pick several sprigs of your herbs in the morning before the dew has dried.

188

Wash carefully and dry on paper towels. Bruise leaves with mortar and pestle to allow oils to emerge.

Bring the best quality red or white wine vinegar to the boiling point. Place the herbs in a vinegar bottle and pour hot vinegar into the bottle, then cork.

Put the bottle in a warm sunny place and shake every 3 days for 1½ weeks. Strain, putting only the liquid back into the bottle. You can add a fresh herb sprig for decoration.

Alexis Stewart's Giant Brown-Sugar Chocolate-Chip Cookies

Preheat oven to 350°.

Assemble 1½ cups brown sugar, ½ cup white sugar, 1 cup unsalted butter, 2 eggs, 1 teaspoon vanilla, 1¾ cups all-purpose flour, 1 teaspoon salt, 1 teaspoon baking powder, ¾ cup coarsely chopped walnuts, and ¾ cup Nestle's semisweet chocolate chips.

Cream together brown sugar, white sugar, and butter. Beat in eggs and vanilla.

Sift flour, salt, and baking powder together. Add to sugar/egg mixture and blend well.

Stir in walnuts and chocolate chips.

Drop, in 2-tablespoon mounds, onto a buttered cookie sheet. Spread mounds well apart. Bake 8 to 10 minutes until cookies are light brown and a knife inserted in the center comes out clean. Cool on racks. Makes 36 cookies.

Lime ice, a recipe from Nan Mabon, is a frosty summer treat that should be made the night before you plan to serve it.

Assemble ½ cup plus 1 tablespoon sugar, 1½ cups water, ¾ cup fresh lime juice, grated rind of 2 large limes, and 6 large limes with tops and pulp removed (optional).

Make a sugar syrup by dissolving sugar in water over medium heat. Bring to a boil and simmer for 5 minutes. Let cool.

Mix together lime juice, the sugar syrup, and the grated rind, and pour into a metal ice tray (with the dividers removed). Place in the freezer overnight.

When mixture is solidly frozen, place half in the bowl of a food processor or blender, then turn machine on and off rapidly until ice is finely textured and free of lumps. Repeat process with the other half of the mixture. Store in a covered container in the freezer until serving time. If you don't have a blender or food processor, stir mixture with a fork every 2 hours until frozen (this prevents crystals from forming).

To serve: Place the ice in the 6 well-chilled limes or in a glass bowl that has been chilled in the freezer. Serves 6.

THE GRAND FINALE

Lemon Curd Tartlets Topped with Fresh Raspberries

This recipe makes enough dough for 12 lemon curd tartlets

Pastry:

Cut 8 tablespoons unsalted butter and 3 tablespoons margarine into 2 cups all-purpose flour, ½ teaspoon sugar, and ¼ teaspoon salt until mixture resembles coarse bread crumbs.

Gradually add ¼ cup iced water. Press dough into a ball, and wrap in plastic wrap or waxed paper. Refrigerate at least 2 hours before rolling.

Preheat oven to 375°. Roll dough to ⅛-inch thickness. Cut pieces slightly larger than tartlet mold and press into mold. Trim edges, then press pastry down into mold with another tartlet mold. Leave second mold in place during baking to keep the tartlet shell from shrinking.

Bake tartlets for 8 to 10 minutes until golden. Remove from pans and cool before filling.

Lemon curd filling:

Cook 1 cup sugar, 6 lightly beaten egg yolks, and ½ cup freshly squeezed lemon juice over a low flame, stirring constantly. Do not boil. The mixture will thicken to coat the spoon.

Remove mixture from heat. Gradually beat in ½ cup softened butter and 1 tablespoon grated lemon peel. Cool.

When lemon curd is cold, fill 12 small tartlets with the mixture. Garnish with fresh raspberries.

Whipped cream is so easy to make yourself that it is sinful to top fresh strawberries or other fresh fruits with artificial whipped cream.

Beat heavy cream in a bowl until the beater leaves light traces on the surface of the cream, and a bit of cream lifted and dropped on the surface will just retain its shape.

*To make a sweeter **Crème Chantilly,** add a dash of vanilla and confectioners' sugar to taste while beating.*

For a really special dessert topping, add framboise or another fruit-flavored liqueur while beating.

CHRIS MEAD

190

Chocolate-covered pears, a cold dessert of fragrant poached pears with a glossy chocolate coating, look most effective when served in a white compote. This recipe comes from Maurice Moore-Betty.

Assemble 1 cup sugar, 4 cups water, juice of 1 lemon, 2 cinnamon sticks, 4 whole cloves, and 6 firm pears.

In a deep pot dissolve sugar in water. Add lemon juice, cinnamon sticks, and whole cloves and simmer, tightly covered, for 10 to 15 minutes.

Peel pears (preferably Anjou or Comice) carefully, leaving stems intact, and cut a slice off the bottom of each so they stand upright.

Poach pears in the gently boiling sugar syrup until tender, approximately 30 to 40 minutes. Cool pears in syrup and then chill thoroughly overnight.

The next day, melt 4 ounces (4 squares) unsweetened chocolate and 2 ounces (2 squares) semisweet chocolate in a bowl over warm water. Add 4 tablespoons softened butter

and stir until it is melted and the mixture is smooth.

Remove pears from syrup and dry gently with paper towels.

Dip pears in the melted chocolate, and coat evenly (use a spoon if necessary). Lift pears to drain off excess chocolate and arrange on a serving dish. Decorate the top of each pear with a sprig of fresh or crystallized mint.

Pears will keep without the chocolate running off for 36 hours. Serves 6.

CHRISTMAS

Decorating your house for Christmas is only a matter of rethinking and reapplying items you already have in the house. Use your collections of folk art and accessories on the tree or as part of seasonal arrangements. Put juniper berries in the crockery, bundles of cinnamon sticks in a basket, fruit and nuts in a wooden bowl.

In the Southwest the holiday is celebrated with Indian dances on Christmas Eve and rooftops and backyards are decorated with lighted candles placed in paper bags filled with sand.

Above all, keep the decorations natural and inexpensive. Place lots of greenery and colorful ornaments everywhere.

Colorful chicken (right), an early 20th-century toy, is the center of a seasonal arrangement. Santas (opposite) are late 19th-century German decorations.

193

TREES AND TRIMMINGS

There are no rules regarding size, shape, or decoration of Christmas trees. Everything—from a ceiling-scraping evergreen decked out in the finest of antique ornaments to the humblest potted plant arrayed with homemade trimmings—is appropriate and, if well done, very effective.

Before you buy a tree (or any decorations), check your own yard and the nearby countryside to see what is available for free. A large bough or an extra bush from the yard, dressed in fruits, flowers, or other local bounty, may be all you need. Consider, too, a family outing to cut your own tree, or buy a live tree that can be planted outdoors.

Trim with whatever you have at home: Use your collection of antique ornaments if you have one, but remember that traditional wood and straw decorations, fruits and berries, bread-dough shapes you make yourself, and candles can be quite attractive.

Tabletop tree, *easily toted from room to room, is perfect for a small space or city apartment. Handmade paper decorations hang from the tree.*

Antique ornaments, *presents from friends, cookies made from old molds, popcorn, cranberries, and candles decorate the ceiling-tall evergreen in this Vermont house.*

Humble tree, *trimmed with popcorn and cranberries and homemade bread-dough ornaments, costs $5 and took 10 minutes to decorate.*

194

OTTO FENN

FRANK KOLLEOGY

195

HOLIDAY WREATHS

Wreaths handcrafted of pine-cones, herbs, grapevines, twigs, greenery, fabric, even vegetables, are easy to make and will last from one holiday season to the next. Decorate your creations with gaily wrapped boxes, berries, flowers, dried seedpods, fruit, toys, ornaments, candy—the list is endless. For variety, make miniature wreaths to hang on the tree, larger ones for the door or wall.

To make the heart-shaped pinecone wreath demonstrated below by William Jarecki of New York's exotic plant shop Mäd-derlake, you will need a wire floral frame (he used a 14-inch heart), 5 to 6 dozen pine or hemlock cones in a variety of sizes (1 to 1½ inches in length is a good size, available at floral supply shops if you cannot gather them yourself), and light-gauge floral wire cut in pieces 6 to 7 inches long. Be sure to place pinecones on the frame both straight up and sideways.

Dried red peppers *on a wire frame make a festive wreath.*

Pinecone wreath *has been dressed up with a red velvet bow.*

A heart-shaped frame *was used to form this pinecone wreath.*

Dried sandolino wreath *is decorated with yellow yarrow. You can dry plants for wreaths yourself.*

Papier-mâché fruits *were placed among the pinecones to add color to this wreath, formed on a wire frame.*

White pine *and juniper berries, off-set by a large fabric bow, were used to make a favorite Christmas wreath.*

Holly wreath *is a traditional holiday decoration.*

Dog biscuits *for the family pet decorate a wreath hanging near his bowl.*

Dried plants *were intertwined to make this wreath.*

Della Robbia wreath *of balsam includes lady apples, kumquats, sickle pears.*

Grapevine wreath *contains fresh vegetables that are changed seasonally.*

Many herbs, *including rosemary, shown here, can be dried and used for wreaths.*

197

Heart-shaped frame *can be found at floral supply stores. Other shapes are also available.*

Loop wires *through wider end of pinecone and twist closed; attach to frame and twist closed again.*

Fill in frame *with smaller cones until full. For variety, add dried berries, flowers, or dried seedpods.*

HOLIDAY TREATS

Spice Fruit Cake can be kept on hand for last-minute gifts. This, and all the recipes on this page, are by Martha Stewart.

Assemble 1 cup water, 2 cups raisins, 1 cup dark brown sugar, ⅓ cup butter, ½ teaspoon cinnamon, ½ teaspoon allspice, ½ teaspoon salt, ¼ teaspoon nutmeg, 1 teaspoon baking powder, 1 teaspoon baking soda, 2 cups cake flour, 1 cup chopped walnuts, and powdered sugar.

Boil together the first 8 ingredients for 3 minutes. Cool mixture. Sift together baking powder, baking soda, and cake flour.

Stir flour mixture into raisin mixture and beat until well blended. Stir in chopped walnuts.

Bake in a buttered and floured 7-inch tube pan in a preheated 325° oven for 1 hour. Cool on rack; sprinkle with powdered sugar.

Apple Cider Grog *is a warm welcoming drink for holiday parties. Heat*

Sleepy kitten, *curled up on an antique quilt under the tree, has become part of the holiday decorations.*

Antique ornaments *with a nautical theme, fresh fruits, and greenery decorate a mantel in a seacoast town.*

198

BARRY O'ROURKE/ETHAN ALLEN LIVE MAGAZINE

BARRY O'ROURKE/ETHAN ALLEN LIVE MAGAZINE

BARRY O'ROURKE/ETHAN ALLEN LIVE MAGAZINE

1 gallon fresh apple cider with cinnamon sticks and 3 apples studded with cloves until hot. Ladle into a big earthenware bowl. Serves 16 to 20.

Home-baked breads are made from a basic French Bread recipe and twisted into a variety of shapes.

Assemble 1 ounce (½ cake) fresh yeast or 2 packages dry yeast, 3¼ cups warm water, 7 cups Heckers or King Arthur unbleached white flour, 4¼ teaspoons salt.

Soften yeast in ½ cup warm water. Mix flour and salt in a large bowl. Add 2¾ cups warm water and mix well. Add the yeast mixture, blend into dough.

Turn onto a floured board and knead until dough is smooth and elastic. Put kneaded dough into a covered bowl and let rise until doubled in bulk. Punch dough down and let rise a second time until doubled. Punch down. Turn onto a floured board.

This will make 6 baguettes, 2 braided loaves, or 6 small couronne (crowns). After forming the loaves, let rise covered with plastic wrap until doubled in size. Baguettes must be slashed along top.

Bake in a preheated 400° oven for 25 minutes. To obtain a fine crust, spray the loaves with water 3 or 4 times during baking. Loaves are done when golden brown and crispy.

Cranberry Tart is a festive dessert for a holiday dinner.

199

A VERMONT CHRISTMAS

"So many of our feelings about Christmas stem from childhood," recalls Gayle Young. "We feel we have to do a traditional, old-fashioned holiday—it wouldn't be Christmas if we didn't." Gayle and partner Daryl Dodson, who own this 18th century house, celebrate with an annual party featuring punch and home-baked favorites. Yearly, too, they cut the tree in the surrounding countryside, and decorate it with antique ornaments and gifts from friends.

200

CHRIS MEAD

Holiday wreath *was handmade of pinecones gathered in the woods.*
Candlelight *in the windows and a wreath on the door promise the welcoming cheer inside this restored 18th-century Cape Cod-style house in New England.*

CHRIS MEAD

Yuletide festivities *start in the dining room, where hot mulled wine and a buffet of fruit cake and other tempting desserts are served on redware.*

CHRISTMAS AT OUR HOUSE

The Emmerling family doesn't leave New York for the holidays anymore. Instead, we take advantage of the city's spectacles—Rockefeller Center's tree, a ride in a hansom cab, the animated department store windows—and recreate a country Christmas in our city apartment. Abundant greenery, cookies and candy canes, popcorn and cranberries, and, especially, a multitude of candles bring welcome country cheer to our city apartment.

Candles first helped me experience the beauty of Christmas, and

202

Painted checkerboards, *hung like portraits, are reasonably priced antique alternatives to paintings.*

Game boards *are 19th- and 20th-century collectibles. Artwork is dressed up for the holidays.*

Carved and painted *wooden watermelon slice on the mantel is by Miles Carpenter. Wreath above is made from twined twigs and fruit.*

I place them all over the house. For holders, I use a variety of unassuming, yet decorative, objects—small tin ashtrays, cookie cutters, and candy molds—that add to the holiday spirit.

Greenery is used everywhere: around the many checkerboards we use as artwork, over a sampler, or just arranged in a basket. There is a large tree, of course, but my favorite decoration is a small $2 tree hung with simple bread-dough ornaments.

Our children, Samantha and Jonathan, join in the decorating too. They help bake cookies, then I leave bowls of candy canes, apples, and gingerbread men around for the children to hang (or eat) as they see fit. And if one of these edible ornaments should break, no tears are shed. We even try to get our dog Piper into the

203

FRANK KOLLEOGY

Christmas colors *of red and green stand out against white living room. Red-and-green appliqúed pillows on the sofa, bowls of red apples and cranberries, candy canes, lots of glowing red candles, and greenery are used for accents.*

fun, with a red-and-green bow around his neck, a stocking, and a wreath decorated with dog biscuits above his bowl.

Samantha and Jonathan also help prepare for the entertaining that is part of the Emmerling Christmas tradition. A party in the kitchen features childhood favorites—cake, cookies, popcorn, fruit, and nuts—that please adults as well. And for more grown-up events, such as our annual Christmas Eve dinner, I serve ham, cheese, crudités—food I try to have on hand throughout the season for impromptu parties. If you keep organized, you can entertain last-minute guests—who often show up in this busy season—without restocking. And with well-worn country pieces, you don't have to polish the wood after every gathering.

Above all, Christmas at our house is a time for togetherness: for being with the children (especially important when both parents work), and for sharing and giving with friends. I love to surprise people. I know what my friends like, and if I see something during the year that they would appreciate, I buy it. Then everyone comes to my house on Christmas to exchange gifts.

Decorative arrangements *of accessories spread the joy of Christmas throughout the house. Here, the front entrance is decorated with a watermelon by contemporary folk artist Felipe Archuleta, a toy Teddy bear, cinnamon sticks, and berries.*

FRANK KOLLEOGY

Child's play: *Samantha Emmerling strings popcorn and cranberries (below) for the tree. At left, she has arranged tea for her Teddy bears (and their friends) under the large pine.*

Hand-painted china *collection is stored in an old pine cupboard. During the holidays the bowls hold shiny ornaments and pomander balls.*

Primitive wooden stepladder *is used during Christmas to display edible goodies, candles, and old toys.*

205

Candy canes *and a toy bear fill our dog Piper's stocking. It is a touch of humor and bright color in the kitchen, where it hangs over his bowl.*

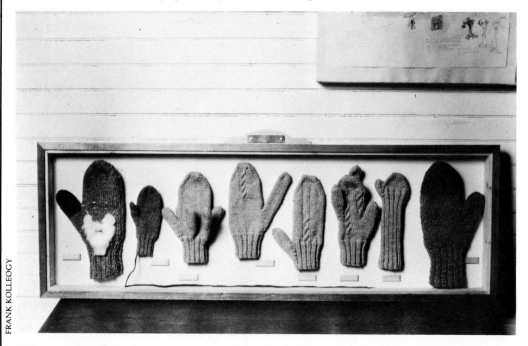

FRANK KOLLEOGY

Antique pine horse *was stripped, mounted as sculpture, and provided with Teddy bear riders and eyeglasses for its "nearsighted condition."*

206

FRANK KOLLEOGY

Mitten display *in a museum case includes mittens that depict different personalities—someone who is "all thumbs," for example—and some from Simpson's past.*

YULETIDE WHIMSY

The whimsical paintings, sculpture, furniture, and three-dimensional displays that artist Tommy Simpson makes and uses throughout his house create a Christmastime atmosphere that lasts throughout the year. While some of the objects shown here have been trimmed for the holidays (note the Santa Claus beard on the mitten below), all the arrangements, from the sleigh bells on the door to the Teddy bears on the antique wooden horse, are permanent decorations.

Playful, joyful, and undeniably humorous, much of Simpson's work harks back to the past—both to his own personal life and to the motifs and materials common to this country's history. "Fanny's Farm," the miniature barnyard scene, originally conceived as a Christmas gift for a friend, is constructed of old wood and is decorated with a Gabriel weather vane, similar to one that would have topped a country barn in the 18th or 19th century. And the mitten collection Simpson designed (left) includes, among the more fanciful examples, a mitten that his mother knit for him when he was a small child.

The rest of the furnishings of Simpson's house—a converted garage of an early 20th-century estate—also demonstrates his interest in the past and in the handmade. Old country pieces—a pie safe, jelly cupboard, oak chairs—are used with furniture of his own design and with plates, glassware, and accessories made by other contemporary craftspeople.

"Fanny's Farm" *was made as a gift for a friend. Note the bird's nest and boot in the barn, the elephant and zebra among the antique and newly carved more common barnyard animals.*

Sleigh bells *that once belonged to Simpson's grandmother and great-aunt hang on the wooden door. Simpson made the patchwork star. The artist's work is shown at Nardin Gallery in New York City.*

207

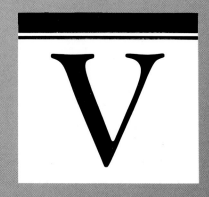

P A R T V

211

COUNTRY COLLECTIONS

The country antiques and collectibles presented in this section can be found at flea markets, antiques shops and shows, auctions, through specialized dealers, even at tag sales. Antiques publications can guide you to country sources in your area. If you can afford to, buy the best. If not, start small, seeking out the less expensive pieces that appeal to you, then later "trading up," selling those objects to buy something more desirable.

"Living" museums—restored houses and even whole towns—offer an excellent opportunity to learn about both the material objects of the past that we now collect and about the ways of life of our American ancestors. Shown here are living museums, each one preserving the cultural heritage of its region.

PERSONAL COLLECTIONS

In the recent past, collectors concentrated on certain very specific areas of Americana: silver, pewter, 18th-century furniture. Today, these fields are out of reach for the average buyer, and the once-ignored objects of the past—bottles, kitchen utensils, rag dolls, to name a few—have become "hot" collectibles.

Things to collect are as varied as the interests of the people who collect them. Collections can be started on the basis of your job, where you live, your hobbies, your pets, or simply a favorite motif, such as hearts or stars. Particularly suited to the country house are all forms of folk art and other unpretentious, handmade

Old bottles, *made since 1739, were commonly for beer, water, medicine, and perfume. Whether bought or dug up in junkyards, the most valuable are colorful and unusually shaped.*

items whose simple forms and sense of the past blend well with primitive furnishings.

What makes your collection appear important, aside from its inherent value, is the way it is displayed. A single bottle, for example, does not have the visual impact of the windowful at left. A single old tool simply looks used, but a collection arranged on a table or hung on the wall makes an important—and personal—decorating statement. Gather together all your bottles, hearts, or antique kitchen utensils and you may discover a collection you never knew you owned.

213

Antique tools—*axes, hammers, anvils, knives, and planes—are found at flea markets. Both hand- and factory-made tools are popular collectibles.*

214

Turn-of-the-century *and contemporary decoys, both floaters and stickup shore-birds, are displayed on a North Shore dresser, c. 1760. The long-beaked curlew stickup decoys were made by craftsman Dick Morgan.*

Cornhusks *wrapped with wire were used to make these new wooden-headed decoys, available for $28 each from Williams Sonoma in Emeryville, Calif. This type of decoy is made today for use as a decorative accessory.*

WILDFOWL DECOYS

Colonial settlers learned about decoys from American Indians. Over the years, decoys became more realistic and two forms developed: floating, for larger fowl, and stickups, for the smaller shorebirds. Floating decoys are still made and used today.

Shorebirds *and floaters were made by contemporary artist R. C. Orcutt.*

Swan decoy *was carved by artist Tom Langan. Both antique and new birds are sold by folk art dealers.*

"Stickup" decoys *were set in the ground on the edge of the water where shorebirds gathered to find food.*

Decoy collection *includes a group of black-bellied plovers from Long Island, c. 1910, in the center, a turn-of-the-century Canada goose from Nova Scotia (far left), and a New England "root head" swan, c. 1870 (far right).*

Old and new decoys *can be found at flea markets and antiques shows. Most were made by anonymous carvers or by decoy factories from the mid-19th century to the 1920s.*

216

Welsh cupboard, *made of pine in the 18th century, holds designer Bill Blass's collection of mochaware decorated with a blue "seaweed" pattern. Mochaware was made in both England and the United States in the 19th century.*

Redware plates, *pitchers, molds, and stoneware fruits are displayed in an early 19th-century open cupboard.*

Redware collection *includes plates decorated with sgraffito, a design cut through one layer to another of contrasting color.*

POTTERY

American pottery was made anywhere there was clay of suitable quality and enough wood to fire the kilns. Redware, glazed with lead, is the oldest native pottery, and decorated examples, as well as decorated salt-glazed stoneware (made after 1825), are most highly valued by collectors. Yellowware, white earthenware, and spongeware are other forms of American pottery collected today.

Bennington ware, *c. 1849, is also known as Rockingham pottery, a form of yellowware glazed with brown.*

217

Black-glazed *redware from New England shares a cupboard with antique woodenware.*

218

Rag dolls, *handmade, c. 1820, are from different areas of New England. The hatted girl from Maine (second from right) is dressed in homespun fabric. Painted toy wagon from the early 20th century holds "Brownie" dolls, named after their designer, of the same period.*

DELIGHTFUL DOLLS

Dolls are not just for children anymore. These playthings of the past and present are now important collectibles, as coveted by adults as by children. While the bisque dolls, which were imported from Europe, are considered by many to be the aristocrats of the doll world, simpler rag or wood dolls were more common.

The first American dolls were made at home of wood or rags,

Contemporary doll *by craftswoman Linda Carr sits beside two old Black rag dolls on a c. 1850 Windsor settee.*

"Mammy" dolls, *made of rags, are on display beneath a 19th-century "Schoolhouse" quilt cover.*

generally unbleached cotton or linen stuffed with sawdust. Their features were hand painted, and often their hair, arranged in the style of the period, is a clue to their age.

The handmade doll is a form of folk art, highly valued by collectors. Not all the antique rag and wooden dolls available today were handmade, however. Starting in the mid-19th century, they were commercially produced as well. While this may lessen their value to folk art collectors, doll collectors still consider them desirable. And many also include new dolls, available at craft shows and shops, in their collections.

New England rag dolls *from the 19th century, each one unique, were handmade from bits and pieces of old clothing out of the scrap bag. These toys, once the peasants of the doll world, are now sold at antiques shows and shops.*

Stuffed toys—*animals, black figures, Santa Claus—were made in the late 19th century of printed cloth that could be cut out, sewn at home, and then stuffed. The toys are sitting on a child's church pew, c. 1820–1830.*

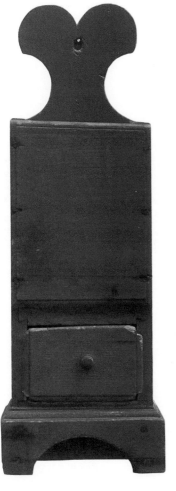

Wooden boxes *to store household necessities were common in the Early American home. This 19th-century hanging box was made to hold pipes.*
Candle sconce *(below) was made of tin in the 19th century. Sconces were used to reflect the candle's light as well as to protect the flame from drafts.*

THE HEART IN THE HOME

The heart is one of the most popular folk art symbols, a timeless motif used in all mediums and, although frequently associated with Pennsylvania Germans, it appears in all parts of this country as well as abroad. The meaning of the heart shape varies from culture to culture. Sometimes it is a purely decorative device, a simple geometric form pleasing to both craftsman and buyer.

221

Large-size heart *(opposite page), a painted pine bank from a 1950s Heart Fund campaign, has become backyard sculpture.*
Cast-iron targets, *once used in early 20th-century shooting galleries, are now collectibles. A frequent sight at carnivals and amusement parks, many targets were scrapped for iron during the two world wars. Remaining targets are more valuable if they are painted or are unusual shapes.*

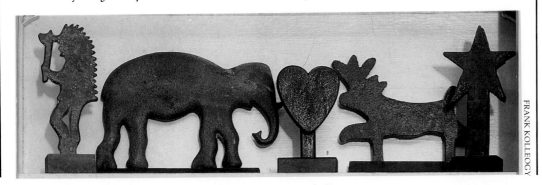

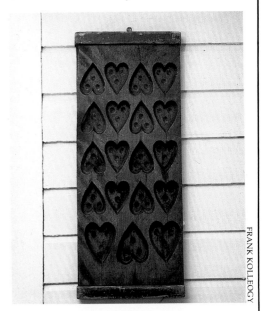

Maple sugar mold, *a mid-19th-century antique, now hangs on the wall as folk art. Wooden molds were also made for cakes, butter, and cigars.*

MUSEUMS

There is no better way to understand how our American ancestors lived—and to see the furnishings they lived with—than to visit the type of "living" museum presented in this section. Instead of static assemblages of objects, these restored houses include working demonstrations and explanations of the daily activities of the early colonists and pioneers, providing a past-century atmosphere as well as an educational experience.

Visits to museums will acquaint you with the finest of country antiques and folk art, yardsticks against which you can measure the merchandise available on the market today. Some museums have side-by-side displays so you can compare period and regional stylistic differences. Some also have pieces of furniture turned upside down, even taken apart, to study the construction.

Museum rooms and displays can also help you see how furnishings and tools were used, and provide a guide for arranging your own country pieces and identifying the often esoteric-looking items found at flea markets.

A listing of museums with collections of country furnishings and folk art starts on page 245.

223

Shaker Village, *containing authentically furnished Shaker buildings and craft demonstrations, is located in Kentucky. Shown here are the water and bath houses, part of one of the first water systems in the state.*

Farm wagon *stands in a field at Shaker Village in Pleasant Hill, Ky., a restored 19th-century community where Shakers once farmed thousands of acres.*

CHRIS MEAD

PRIMED WITH COLOR

The Stencil House, part of Vermont's Shelburne Museum, is most noted for its well-preserved stencil decoration. Painted directly on wooden boards 10 to 20 years after the house was built in 1790, the work is in the style of itinerant artist Moses Eaton. Other rooms are painted green.

Dry sink, *lined with metal, was used for washing dishes. Hanging at left is an old wooden washboard.*

Stencil designs, *painted directly on the boards, possibly by Moses Eaton, were preserved under wallpaper.*

Green-painted *walls and wide-board floors reveal the Early American's love of color. In the center of the kitchen is an 18th-century tavern-type table with a scrubbed pine top, holding an unusually large pewter bowl.*

224

CHRIS MEAD

225

226

Trundle bed *slides out from under a large press bed in this family-sized bedroom. Trundle beds often had wheels to allow them to be easily rolled under other beds, and they were usually made for children. They were very popular in the 19th century. The ropes visible at the ends and sides of the beds on these pages were the mattress "springs" of the past, as a network of ropes held the bed together. Pegs on the wall hold the family's clothes since early houses had no closets.*

Press beds *(or folding beds—the forerunner of Murphy beds) had hinged rails that folded upward, allowing them to be stored in a press (cupboard) or closet. The variation of this style at right was not meant to be stored in a cupboard, but has a simple, high canopy frame into which the rear of the bed folds. The curtains are then drawn closed, hiding the bed. Two contrasting homespun plaids were used here for the canopy and the bed covering.*

BEDROOMS AT SHELBURNE

Vermont's Shelburne Museum is composed of 36 buildings, many of them historic structures, filled with fine collections of Americana. Founded in 1947 by Electra Havermeyer Webb and her husband, J. Watson Webb, the museum first housed the Webbs' extensive personal collections. Over the years, other collections were donated to the museum, and buildings of historic importance were moved, some piece by piece, to Shelburne. Shown here are several bedrooms in the museum.

Six-legged press bed *with side rails hinged at the middle set of legs is an early 18th-century style.*

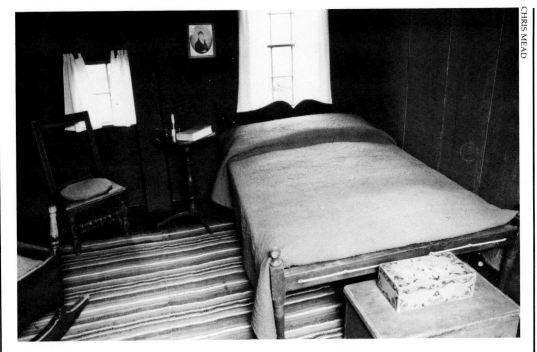

Low-post bed *with cupid's bow headboard stands in the east chamber of Shelburne's late 18th-century Stencil House (above). The bed is covered with an elaborately stitched red quilt in linsey-woolsey, a coarse cloth made of linen and wool.*

Under-eaves, *or low-post, beds, common from 1700 to 1840, may, as the name implies, have originally been used in the corners of attic rooms or wherever a low roof limited the height of the posts. This bed (below) is covered with a diamond patterned quilt.*

227

STUDY HALLS

The Winedale Historical Center in Round Top, Texas, is an educational branch of the University of Texas at Austin, used as a center for the study of the ethnic cultures of central Texas. The 190-acre farmstead, the original house on the property and its outbuildings, all restored to their 19th-century condition, were donated to the university by Houston philanthropist Ima Hogg in 1967. Since then, three more historic buildings—simple cottages and a large Greek Revival farmhouse—have been

moved to the site and restored.

The history of the farm dates to 1831, when the Mexican government granted the land to William S. Townsend, an Austin colonist. The house and land were sold in 1848 to Samuel Lewis, who expanded the building and developed the property. In the 1880s, house and outbuildings were purchased by Joseph George Wagner, a German immigrant to Round Top. Descendants of Wagner's family lived here until 1961, when Miss Hogg bought the farm and started restoration work.

Pine bed, *c. 1870, in an 1850s frame cottage, was made in Texas. The quilt is also from the 19th century.*
High wheel spinning wheel, *c. 1810, spun wool and cotton.*

229

A LEARNING EXPERIENCE

Because of its emphasis on regional decorative arts, most of the furnishings at Winedale Historical Center were made in Texas, many by the Anglo-American and German cabinetmakers active in central Texas in the mid-19th century. Winedale is primarily an educational institution, but tours are given for the public on weekends.

Elm and cedar bed, *made in Texas in 1850, is covered with a 19th-century quilt. The walls of this c. 1855 cottage still show the original paint and stenciling.*

Decorated stairway *stands in a typical 1850s Texas farm building.*
Rocking chair *and blanket chest are from early 18th-century Pennsylvania.*

231

MOUNTAIN SPIRIT

The Arwine Cabin, part of the Museum of Appalachia in Norris, Tenn., is a one-room log structure built about 1800 in Arwine Town, Tenn., and moved to the museum by its founder, John Irwin. The yellow poplar building with its rough, puncheon floor was actually occupied until 1936, although Irwin has furnished it in a manner consistent with its early 19th-century heritage.

CHRIS MEAD

A front porch *was a common and essential storage space for log cabins.*

Also shown here is the front porch of the General Bunch House, one of the newest buildings in the museum complex, built c. 1890. It comes from Anderson County, Tenn., a region settled nearly a hundred years later than other parts of the state, and where pioneer conditions prevailed much longer. The large barrels on the porch—they each hold over 200 gallons—were made from black gum trees and used to store grain, corn, or wheat.

Arwine Cabin *furnishings include a late 18th-century corner cupboard and a cowhide-topped chest, papered inside with 1830 Baltimore newspapers, brought to Appalachia by pioneers.*

233

Appalachian rocker *has a woven hickory bark seat and a maple frame.*

OUR PIONEER PAST

For more than 20 years, John Rice Irwin, founder of the Museum of Appalachia in Norris, Tenn., has traveled backwoods paths and unpaved roads, seeking old tools, kitchen utensils, furniture, and other "primitives," handmade by the mountain people of the Appalachian region.

"My great respect and admiration for these people sparked my interest in collecting relics depicting their history," says Irwin. He

234

Broom making *is demonstrated in the Broom and Rope House. Broomcorn was grown by almost every family in Appalachia, and in the early days everyone made his own round brooms.*

Wooden stairway *separates the two rooms of the saddlebag cabin.*

Underground dairy *is used to store milk products. Covered with sod for insulation, this type of structure is called a root cellar in the Midwest.*

Preserves and pickles *stand in the simple, handmade cupboard of the General Bunch House, c. 1890. The fireplace in this one-room log cabin is unusual because of its self-supporting arch. Wood rocker is in a country Queen Anne style.*

was started in his collecting by his grandfather, who had a profound appreciation for his pioneer ancestors. He also had an accumulation of primitive items spanning three or four generations.

To house his collection, which now includes some 40,000 frontier and pioneer relics, Irwin moved 13 log cabins to a new site in rural Tennessee, and reconstructed and furnished them in an authentic style. Besides restored residences, Irwin's "living mountain village" includes a blacksmith shop, corn-grinding mill, smokehouse, broom and rope factory, and other buildings that illustrate the self-sufficient way of life of the hardy mountaineers.

235

Dirt floor cabin, *typical of early frontier houses, was built in Anderson County, Tenn., c. 1840. Red clay and straw "chinking" fills the cracks between the logs.*

Wood shakes *are cut by hand to cover the cabin roofs.*

Seed Shop exhibit *contains large seed bins, Shaker seed boxes, a bluegrass seed rake, and sieves used to separate different sizes of seed, all mid-19th-century artifacts. Selling seeds was an important Shaker trade.*

236

SHAKER SIMPLICITY

According to their religion, nothing the Shakers made could be ornamented. With every trace of decoration eliminated from their designs, the beauty of their craftsmen's work emerged from its clean lines and proportions. Their accomplishments are prized as classics of American design.

Today, in Shaker communities such as Shaker Village in Pleasant Hill, Ky., visitors can see examples of Shaker craftsmanship in authentic settings and watch demonstrations of how the furniture, boxes, and other items were made.

Ladder-back chair, *referred to as a "common chair" in the Shaker community, was made c. 1830 and is original to Pleasant Hill. The adjustable lit candle sconce, made of cherry, is also from the early 19th century.*

Peg racks *surrounded the walls of all Shaker buildings to hold clothes, furniture and accessories.*

Herbs *were used by the Shakers to make moth repellent bags.*

At Shaker Village, one can also visit the buildings that many consider the pinnacle of Shaker design. Built by master architect and carpenter Micajah Burnett, they combine early New England Shaker building forms with Federal classicism.

Twenty-seven buildings are open to the public, including craft shops, dwellings, and the Trustees House, where guest rooms and dining facilities are located.

Willow basket *was used at Pleasant Hill as an herb carrier. The smaller basket was made for sale to outsiders.*

Summer meals *at Pleasant Hill might have consisted of the foods shown here— biscuits, breads, corn sticks, angel food cake, fresh vegetables, salt-cured country ham, and Shaker lemon pie. Hearty meals are still served at the Trustees House.*

237

Hanging cupboard, *an example of Shaker craftsmanship, was made at the Pleasant Hill community in 1830. Also hanging on pegs are a basket, a sheaf of dried wheat, and a revolving trivet from the early 19th century.*

238

THE WILD WEST

Henkel Square Restoration is composed of fourteen buildings, including an apothecary shop, general meetinghouse, church, smokehouse, and a weaving house, as well as residences. All the structures were moved to the site from locations in Round Top and surrounding towns; the farthest one from 20 miles away.

Horse blanket *on the floor was used under a saddle during the day; placed in front of the fire at night. Windows are bare since material was scarce on the frontier.*

Writing desk *was made in Grapevine, Tex., in the early 1850s.*
Stenciling *on walls was done by German immigrants in the mid-19th century. Walnut bed is from Texas.*

239

HANDMADE IN TEXAS

The houses at Henkel Square Restoration in Round Top, Tex., are examples of true frontier architecture. Some are simple one- or two-room log cabins; others are larger, but all exhibit the superb hand-crafting of the early German settlers in the area. Inside, the restoration is as authentic as possible. Walls are still covered with the original stencils, paint, or paper. Seen here are the "wash bluing" (bleach for clothes, dissolved in white paint to add a blue color)

walls of the Muckelroy house (right) and the painted walls of the Schuhmann house (below). Almost all the furnishings in all the houses were made locally in Texas in the early or mid-19th century. Exceptions include the imported china and ironstone, and other "exotic" items that would have been sold in Mr. Henkel's general store during the period. Also imported to Texas were the few pieces of furniture the pioneers brought with them, such as the West Virginia walnut bed in the Muckelroy house that came by wagon train.

Pine wardrobe was made in Texas by immigrants. The rocker was also made locally in the early 19th century.

240

CHRIS MEAD

Bedroom furnishings *in the Schuhmann house are few and simple in design: a walnut-and-pine bed, a plain table, a ladder-back chair with cowhide seat. All were made in Texas in the early 19th century.*

241

242

TEXAS TRADITION

Henkel Square Restoration in Round Top, Tex., was founded in the early 1960s by Mr. and Mrs. Charles L. Bybee as an authentic representation of the way of life of the early German immigrant settlers in Texas. The late Mr. Bybee, a fourth-generation Texan, was impressed by both the fine houses and the arduous existence of these pioneers, and felt that their

Texas-made furnishings *from the 1840s fill the Muckelroy log house.*
One-room cabin *was built of oak logs in 1840.*

Pitcher and bowl *were kept on the front porch for washing up. This set dates from the mid-19th century.*

heritage—their buildings and furnishings as well as the memory of their difficult life—was worthy of preservation. Today the restoration includes the houses of several German immigrants who settled in the area before the Civil War. The Bybees named their restoration "Henkel Square" after the German merchant who founded Round Top.

243

244

Directory of Museums and Restorations

The *Directory of Museums and Restorations* lists 150 major museums, re-created villages, individual historic houses, and pioneer log cabins. It is a sampling rather than a complete assemblage of the many museums and restorations available to those who would like to have a closer look at Early American furniture, arts, and life. These places range in size and types of collections, but each has an important story to tell about the history of our country and the heritage of its many inhabitants.

NEW ENGLAND

Connecticut

Farmington Museum
37 High Street
Farmington, Conn. 06032
(203)677–9222
Historic Stanley-Whitman House of 1660, with period furnishings and exhibits of local history, a lean-to addition, display room with changing exhibitions, flower and herb gardens with 17th- and 18th-century planting materials.

Putnam Cottage
243 East Putnam Avenue
Greenwich, Conn. 06830
(203)869–9697
Historic house built in 1690 and used by General Israel Putnam during Revolutionary War with exhibits of local history.

The Guilford Keeping Society
Boston Street
Guilford, Conn. 06437
(203)453–3176
1736 house, with exhibits of local history, documents, and costumes.

Henry Whitfield State Historical Museum
Old Whitfield Street
Guilford, Conn. 06437
(203)453–2457
Oldest dwelling in New England, built in 1639, with 17th- and 18th-century furnishings.

Hyland House
84 Boston Street
Guilford, Conn. 06437
(203)453–9477
House built 1660, with period furnishings.

Mystic Seaport
Route 27/Greenmanville Road
Mystic, Conn. 06355
(203)536–2631
Seventeen-acre maritime museum containing re-created 19th-century seacoast community with working craftsmen, preservation shipyard, 4 major historic vessels, and formal museum display buildings.

Hempstead House
Hempstead Street
New London, Conn. 06320
(203)443–7949
Historic 17th-century house, with appropriate furnishings.

Nathan Hale Homestead
South Street
South Coventry, Conn. 06238
(203)742–6917
Ten-room Georgian-style house built in 1776, with period furnishings.

Stratford Historical Society Museum
967 Academy Hill
Stratford, Conn. 06497
(203)378–0630
Historic Judson House built 1723, with period furnishings and local history exhibits.

Buttolph-Williams House
249 Broad Street
Wethersfield, Conn. 06109
(203)529–0460
House built 1692, with period furnishings and kitchen equipment.

Webb-Deane-Stevens Museum
211 Main Street
Wethersfield, Conn. 06109
(203)529–7371
Complex of 3 authentically restored 18th-century houses, with early furniture and decorative arts collections.

Wethersfield Historical Society
150 Main Street
Wethersfield, Conn. 06109
(203)529–7656
House built 1804, with exhibits of local history, household and farm implements. The society also maintains 3 other dwellings: John Hurlbutt House, James Francis House, and Old Warehouse.

The Windsor Historical Society and Wilson Museum
96 Palisade Avenue
Windsor, Conn. 06095
(203)688–3813
Historic Fyler house of 1640, with period furnishings and local history displays.

Maine

Parson Smith Homestead
River Road
South Windham, Maine 04082
(207)892–5315
Historic 8-room house built in 1764, with furnishings.

Massachusetts

Colonel John Ashley House˙
Cooper Hill Road
Ashley Falls, Mass. 01222
(413)229–8600
House built in 1765, with 18th-century period furnishings and herb garden.

Museum of Fine Arts
479 Huntington Avenue
Boston, Mass. 02115
(617)267–9300
M. and M. Karolik Collections of American folk art and primitive paintings.

Paul Revere House
19 North Square
Boston, Mass. 02116
(617)523–1676
Historic house of 1680, with period furnishings.

Society for the Preservation of New England Antiquities
141 Cambridge Street
Boston, Mass. 02114
(617)227–3956
Located in 1795 Harrison Gray Otis House, with displays of regional decorative arts, architectural prints, photographs, toys, and needlework. The society maintains historic houses in Massachusetts, Maine, New Hampshire, Connecticut, and Rhode Island.

Concord Museum
Route 2A/Lexington Road and Cambridge Turnpike
Concord, Mass. 01742
(617)369–9609

Period rooms, Emerson study, Thoreau room, diorama of the Battle of Concord, herb garden.

Orchard House
Route 2A/399 Lexington Road
Concord, Mass. 01742
(617)369–4118
Alcott family home during the 19th century; consisting of 2 combined houses built in 1650 and 1730.

Ralph Waldo Emerson House
28 Cambridge Turnpike
Concord, Mass. 01742
(617)369–2236
House built in 1828, with original period furnishings.

The Fairbanks House
East Street and
Eastern Avenue
Dedham, Mass. 02026
(617)326–1170
Oldest wood frame house in United States, inhabited from 1636 to 1903, with family furnishings.

Historic Deerfield
The Street
Deerfield, Mass. 01342
(413)773–8689
Twelve house-museums with period furnishings.

"Beauport" Museum
Eastern Point Boulevard
Gloucester, Mass. 01930
(617)283–0800
Collections of American decorative arts.

Porter-Phelps-Huntington House
128 River Drive/Route 47
Hadley, Mass. 01035
(413)584–4699
House built in 1752, with household articles of the 17th, 18th, and 19th centuries.

★ HANCOCK SHAKER/FRANK KOLLEOGY

Hancock Shaker Village ★
U.S. 20
Hancock, Mass. 01237
Mail: Box 898
Pittsfield, Mass. 01201
(413)443–0188
Restored settlement of 21 buildings outfitted with collections of Shaker-made furniture and artifacts, farm buildings, and, most famous of the Village buildings, the Round Stone Barn, built in 1826.

Fruitlands Museums
Prospect Hill
Harvard, Mass. 01451
(617)456–3924
Six buildings with 4 collections: Bronson Alcott's Fruitlands, Shaker House, American Indian Museum, and picture gallery with paintings by the Hudson River School.

Buttonwoods Museum
240 Water Street
Haverhill, Mass. 01830
(617)374–4626
Four houses with a total of 21 authentic rooms: "The Buttonwoods" house of 1814 with household items of the 18th and 19th centuries, Children's Museum, John Ward House, and 19th-century shoe shop.

Hingham Historical Society/
The Old Ordinary
21 Lincoln Street
Hingham, Mass. 02043
(617)749–0013
Historic house of early 18th century, with collections of old tools and woodenware.

Hancock Clarke House
35 Hancock Street
Lexington, Mass. 02173
(617)862–5598
House built in 1698, with 8 period rooms.

Munroe Tavern
1332 Massachusetts Avenue
Lexington, Mass. 02173
(617)862–1703
House built in 1695, with period rooms.

Nantucket Historical Association
Old Town Hall
Union Street
Nantucket, Mass. 02557
(617)228–1894
Housed in the old Town Hall, the association provides information on: 1720 Nathaniel Macy House, 1746 Old Mill, the 1800 House, the 1805 Old Gaol, 1838 Friends Meeting House, the 1845 Greek Revival Hadwen House-Satler Memorial, Whaling Museum, and Peter Foulger Museum.

The Jabez Howland House
33 Sandwich Street
Plymouth, Mass. 02360
(617)746–9590
House built in 1667, with period furnishings.

Plimoth Plantation:
The 1627 Pilgrim Village and Mayflower
P.O. Box 1620
Plymouth, Mass. 02360
(617)746–1622
Living outdoor museum re-creating the life of the early Plymouth settlers.

Plymouth Antiquarian Society
126 Water Street
Plymouth, Mass. 02360
(617)746–9697
Society maintains 3 authentically furnished historic houses: 1747 Spooner House with its headquarters, 1677 Harlow Old Fort House, and 1809 Antiquarian House.

Adams Birthplaces
131 and 141 Franklin Street
Quincy, Mass. 02169
Birthplaces of John Adams and John Quincy Adams.

Adams National Historic Site
135 Adams Street
Quincy, Mass. 02169
(617)773–1177
Adams family residence, with family heirlooms and furniture, garden, and carriage house.

Quincy Homestead
Hancock Street and
Butler Road
Quincy, Mass. 02169
(617)472–1177
Georgian mansion built in 1685, with authentic furnishings, herb gardens, and carriage house.

246

Quincy House
20 Muirhead Street
Quincy, Mass. 02170
(617)472–1587
Merchant's house of 1770,
with furnishings.

Essex Institute
132 Essex Street
Salem, Mass. 01970
(617)744–3390
Collections of early American
decorative arts: clocks,
tools, toys, and paintings.
Also maintains authentic
period houses.

House of Seven Gables
54 Turner Street
Salem, Mass. 01970
(617)744–0991
Three 17th-century houses,
with period furnishings.

Salem Witch House
310½ Essex Street
Salem, Mass. 01970
(617)744–5217
Historic house built in 1692,
home of Magistrate Jonathan
Corwin during witchcraft
trials, with 17th-century
furnishings.

Heritage Plantation
of Sandwich
Grove and Pine Streets
Sandwich, Mass. 02563
(617)888–3300
Three museum buildings
situated on 76 acres of
woodlands and gardens, with
collections of decorative arts,
weapons, and military
miniatures.

Saugus Ironworks
244 Central Street
Saugus, Mass. 01906
(617)233–0050
Buildings from 1646 iron
industry: Iron Master's
house, mills, and forge.

The Mission House
Main and Sargent Streets
Stockbridge, Mass. 01062
(413)298–3383
House built in 1735, with
period furnishings and herb
garden.

Old Sturbridge Village
Sturbridge, Mass. 01566
(617)347–3362
Re-created town illustrating
American life between 1790
and 1840.

New Hampshire
Shaker Village, Inc.
Canterbury, N.H. 03224
(603)783–9822
A village still occupied by
Shaker sisters, with museum
in old meetinghouse of 1742
and guided tours of
additional dwellings.

New Hampshire
Historical Society
30 Park Street
Concord, N.H. 03301
(603)225–3381
Four period rooms with
collections of New
Hampshire decorative arts
and changing exhibits.

The Currier Gallery of Art
192 Orange Street
Manchester, N.H. 03104
(603)669–6144
Exhibits of American
decorative arts, including
pewter, glass, and paintings.

Strawbery Banke, Inc.
P.O. Box 360
Portsmouth, N.H. 03801
(603)436–8010
Preservation of 17th-, 18th-,
and 19th-century seaport
homes.

Vermont
The Bennington Museum
West Main Street
Bennington, Vt. 05201
(802)442–2180
Collections of American
crafts, folk art, furniture,
Grandma Moses paintings,
Early American glass, and
Bennington pottery.

Orleans County
Historical Society
Orleans RFD
Brownington, Vt. 05860
(802)754–2022
Stone house built 1836, with
exhibits of local history and
early farm and household
items.

Sheldon Museum
1 Park Street
Middlebury, Vt. 05753
(802)388–2117
House of 1829, with
collections of pewter, toys,
pottery, 18th- and 19th-
century furnishings, primitive
tools, and 19th-century oil
portraits.

★ SHELBURNE/CHRIS MEAD

Shelburne Museum ★
U.S. 17
Shelburne, Vt. 05482
(802)985–3346
Collections of Americana,
including early American
houses, shops, a steamboat,
covered bridge, folk art
exhibits, textiles, costumes,
dolls, decoys, and toys.

MID-ATLANTIC

Delaware
The Hagley Museum
Greenville
Wilmington, Del. 19807
(302)658–2401
19th-century industrial
community located on
200 acres of wooded land
with museum building, mill
network of buildings and
gardens.

The Corbit Sharp House
Main Street
Odessa, Del. 19730
(302)378–2681
Historic house of 1772, with
period rooms and decorative
arts of the 18th and 19th
centuries.

Henry Francis du Pont
Winterthur Museum and
Gardens
Winterthur, Del. 19735
(302)656–8591
Collections of American
decorative arts from 1640 to
1840, displayed in more than
175 rooms, exhibit areas,
and 60 acres of planted
gardens; with examples of
architecture, furniture,
textiles, and needlepoint.

New Jersey
Monmouth County
Historical Association
70 Court Street
Freehold, N.J. 07728
(201)462–1466
Museum building, with
collections of furniture,
paintings, toys, and
weapons; also maintains
4 historic 18th- and 19th-
century furnished houses.

247

Morristown National
Historic Park
230 Morris Avenue East
Morristown, N.J. 07960
(201)221–0311
Eighteenth-century Ford
Mansion, Wick Farm of 1750,
and 5 reconstructed huts.

Historic Town of Smithville
Smithville, N.J. 08201
(609)652–7777
Re-created mid-19th-century
southern New Jersey town,
with exhibits in 40 buildings;
period furnishings and craft
demonstrations.

Old Dutch Parsonage and
The Wallace House
38 Washington Place
Somerville, N.J. 08876
(201)725–1015
Two 18th-century houses
with appropriate 18th- and
19th-century furnishings.

New York
Historic Cherry Hill
532½ South Pearl Street
Albany, N.Y. 12202
(518)434–4791
Georgian-style house of 1787
situated on 5 acres, with
original furnishings.

Old Bethpage Village
Round Swamp Road
Bethpage, L.I., N.Y. 11804
(516)420–5280
Re-created pre-Civil War
Long Island farming
community.

Brooklyn Museum
188 Eastern Parkway
Brooklyn, N.Y. 11238
(212)638–5000
Four centuries of American
decorative arts displayed in
30 period rooms, with
collections of American
paintings, sculpture, and
American Indian artifacts.

The Farmer's Museum and
The Village Crossroads
Lake Road
Cooperstown, N.Y. 13326
(607)547–2593
Museum exhibits include folk
art, agricultural and
household implements, an
18th-century house, shop,
and church, and craft
demonstrations. The village is
a re-created 18th-century
New York State town.

Fenimore House
Lake Road
Cooperstown, N.Y. 13326
(607)547–2533
Collections of American
folk art, Hudson River
School paintings, and
James Fenimore Cooper
memorabilia.

Boscobel Restoration, Inc.
Route 9D
Garrison, N.Y. 10524
(914)265–3638
New York 19th-century
Federal-style country house,
with period furnishings.

House of History
Route 9
Kinderhook, N.Y. 12106
(518)758–9265
1819 Federal period restoration.

Van Alen House
Route 9H
Kinderhook, N.Y. 12106
(518)758–6988
1737 Dutch farmhouse, with
period furnishings.

Hurley Patentee Manor
RD 7/Box 98A
Kingston, N.Y. 12401
(914)331–5414
Two limestone dwellings:
1696 Dutch-influenced house
and 1745 English Georgian
house, both with period
furnishings and displays.

Museum Village in
Orange County
Museum Village Road
Route 17M
Monroe, N.Y. 10950
(914)782–8247
Outdoor museum of 19th-
century American
technology.

Washington's Headquarters
State Historic Site
84 Liberty Street
Newburgh, N.Y. 12550
(914)562–1195
Hasbrouck House of c. 1750,
with late 18th-century
furnishings.

Huguenot Historical
Society, Inc.
Huguenot Street
New Paltz, N.Y. 12561
(914)255–1660
Seventeenth-century stone
house and French church,
with period furnishings.

Thomas Paine Cottage
North and Paine Avenues
New Rochelle, N.Y. 10802
(914)632–5376
18th-century farmhouse.

Cooper-Hewitt Museum
2 East 91st Street
New York, N.Y. 10028
(212)860–6898
Collections of decorative arts,
including textiles, furniture,
ceramics, glass, woodwork,
drawings, prints,
architectural ornaments,
and American wallpapers
from the 18th century.

Metropolitan Museum of Art
Fifth Avenue at 82nd Street
New York, N.Y. 10011
(212)879–5500
Collections of 18th- and 19th-
century American paintings
and sculpture, and late 17th-
to mid-18th-century period
rooms.

Museum of American
Folk Art
49 West 53rd Street
New York, N.Y. 10019
(212)581–2474
Interpretation and exhibitions
of American folk art from the
late 17th century through the
20th century, with collections
of naïve paintings, carvings,
tools, signs and symbols,
textiles, and pottery reflecting
the inventiveness of the self-
taught artist.

Shaker Museum
Shaker Museum Road
Old Chatham, N.Y. 12136
(518)794–9105
Oldest and largest collection
of Shaker artifacts.

The Kent-DeLord
House Museum
17 Cumberland Avenue
Plattsburgh, N.Y. 12901
(518)561–1035
Historic house of 1797, with
6 period rooms and paintings
by Inman.

Landmarks Society of
Western New York, Inc.
130 Spring Street
Rochester, N.Y. 14608
(716)546–7029
Two house-museums: Stone
Tolan House of 1790 and
Greek Revival Campbell-
Whittlesey House of 1835.

Memorial Art Gallery of
University of Rochester
490 University Avenue
Rochester, N.Y. 14607
(716)275–3081
Collections of American folk
art, paintings, and other
decorative arts.

Richmondtown Restoration
441 Clarke Avenue
Staten Island, N.Y. 10306
(212)351–1611

248

Seven 17th-, 18th-, and 19th-century restored dwellings with period furnishings, and museum building with exhibits of late 18th- and 19th-century tools and machinery.

Sleepy Hollow Restorations: Sunnyside, Philipsburg Manor, Van Cortlandt Manor
Headquarters:
150 White Plains Road
Tarrytown, N.Y. 10591
(914)631–8200
Restorations representing the history of the Hudson River Valley over a span of 3 centuries; each reflects its period and the differing life patterns along the Hudson.

Pennsylvania

Old Economy Village
14th and Church Streets
Ambridge, Pa. 15003
(412)266–4500
Preservation project: houses, shops, and gardens of Harmonist settlement of the early 19th century.

Meadowcroft Village
Avella, Pa. 15312
(412)587–3412
Restored 19th-century rural village, with houses, barns, shops; 15 buildings.

Historic Bethlehem, Inc.
516 Main Street
Bethlehem, Pa. 18018
(215)868–6311
Re-creation and restoration of the 18th- and 19th-century industrial area of Bethlehem.

Daniel Boone Homestead
RD 2
Birdsboro, Pa. 19508
(215)582–4900
Mid-19th-century farmhouse, blacksmith shop, and barn on foundation of birthplace of pioneer.

Brandywine River Museum*
U.S. 1/P.O. Box 141
Chadds Ford, Pa. 19317
(215)388–7601
Museum in a century-old gristmill, with paintings by Wyeth family, Howard Pyle, Maxfield Parrish, Frank Schoonover, and many others.

Wright's Ferry Mansion
38 South Second Street
Columbia, Pa. 17512
(717)684–4325
Restored 1738 period house, with 18th-century Pennsylvania William and Mary, and Queen Anne furniture.

Hopewell Village National Historic Site
RD 1/P.O. Box 345
Elverson, Pa. 19520
(215)582–8773
Restored 18th- and 19th-century ironmaking community.

Historic Fallsington, Inc.
4 Yardley Avenue
Fallsington, Pa. 19054
(215)295–6567

Maintains and preserves 4 historic buildings, all with period furnishings: a 1685 log cabin, 1790 stagecoach tavern, 18th-century Burgess-Lippincott House, and 1758 schoolmaster's house.

William Penn
Memorial Museum
North and 3rd Streets
Harrisburg, Pa. 17120
(717)787–4978
Collections of 17th-, 18th-, 19th-century Pennsylvania decorative arts, with permanent and special exhibits.

Curtin Village Restoration
RD 2
Howard, Pa. 16841
(814)355–3687
Pre-Civil War ironworks, with ironmaster's house and workers' cottages.

Pennsylvania Farm Museum of Landis Valley
2451 Kissel Hill Road
Lancaster, Pa. 17601
(717)569–0401
Three separate farms, spanning the centuries from the pioneer era to the

Victorian age, with exhibits of folk art, crafts, and farm implements.

Frank McCoy House
17 North Main Street
Lewistown, Pa. 17044
(717)242–1022
Early 19th-century house, with original furnishings.

Pennsbury Manor
Route 9
Morrisville, Pa. 19067
(215)946–0400
Re-creation of William Penn's 18th-century country manor, with period furnishings.

Joseph Priestly House
472 Priestly Avenue
Northumberland, Pa. 17857
(717)473–9474
Eighteenth-century house, with furnishings and original artifacts.

Philadelphia Museum of Art
26th Street and Benjamin Franklin Parkway
Philadelphia, Pa. 19103
(215)763–8100
Collections include Pennsylvania German artifacts, the "Millbach" Pennsylvania German kitchen, naïve paintings from the Garbisch Collection, and Shaker artifacts.

Morton Homestead
100 Lincoln Avenue
Prospect Park, Pa. 19076
(215)583–7221
Swedish-style log house of the 17th century.

Robert Fulton Birthplace
RD 1/U.S. 222 and Swift Road
Quarryville, Pa. 19566
(717)548–2679
Restoration of 18th-century farmhouse, with period furnishings.

249

David Bradford House
175 South Main Street
Washington, Pa. 15301
(412)222–3604
House built c. 1794, with
period furnishings.

Conrad Weiser Park
RD 1/U.S. 422
Womelsdorf, Pa. 19567
(215)589–2934
Stone house built c. 1755,
with park.

Washington, D.C.
National Gallery of Art
Constitution Avenue at
6th Street N.W.
Washington, D.C. 20565
(202)737–4215
Edgar William and Bernice
Chrysler Garbisch Collection
of folk art; also additional
collections of 18th- and 19th-
century American oil
paintings, drawings, and
watercolors.

Smithsonian Institution
Washington, D.C. 20560
(201)381–5855
Collection and exhibitions
housed in several buildings,
among them:
Freer Gallery of Art:
Collections of 19th- and early
20th-century American
works, which include
paintings by Whistler,
Winslow Homer, Albert
Pinkham Ryder, and John
Singer Sargent.
National Museum of History
and Technology:
Collections include folk art,
clocks, tools, textiles, and
ceramics.
National Collection of
Fine Arts:
Collections of American
paintings, sculpture, and
graphic art from the 18th
century to the present.

Renwick Gallery:
Changing exhibitions of
contemporary and historic
American crafts, decorative
arts, and design, with
principal rooms restored
and refurnished in the style
of the late 19th century.

THE SOUTH

Alabama
The Fine Arts Museum
of the South
Museum Drive
Mobile, Ala. 36608
(205)342–4642
Collections of 19th- and
20th-century American
paintings and prints,
sculpture, Southern
decorative arts from c. 1810
to 1860, and 19th-century
lighting.

Florida
San Augustin Antiquo
P.O. Box 1987
Saint Augustine, Fla. 32084
(904)824–6383
Restored 18th-century
Spanish colonial village, with
craft demonstrations.

Georgia
High Museum of Art
1280 Peachtree Street N.W.
Atlanta, Ga. 30309
(404)892–3600
Collections of 18th- to
20th-century American
paintings, decorative arts,
and furniture.

Kentucky
Shaker Village at
Pleasant Hill
Route 4
Harrodsburg, Ky. 40330
(606)734–5411
Restored 19th-century
Shaker village with 27

original buildings on 3,000
acres of farmland; includes
furnished dwellings, shops,
meetinghouse, post office,
craft demonstrations, and
overnight accommodations
available in restored
dwellings.

Duncan Tavern
Historic Center
Public Square/Highway 68
Paris, Ky. 40361
(606)987–1788
Two historic buildings:
a tavern and dwelling,
both with period furnishings.

Maryland
Hammond-Harwood House
19 Maryland Avenue
Annapolis, Md. 21401
(301)269–1714
Historic house built
in 1774 by colonial
architect William Buckland,
with period furnishings.

Southerly Mansion
Hollywood, Md. 20636
(301)373–3280
Eighteenth-century manor
house, with working
plantation.

North Carolina
Historic Edenton
Edenton, N.C. 27932
(919)482–3663
Five restored 18th- and 19th-
century buildings: 3 houses
with period furnishings, a
courthouse and church still
in use.

Museum of Early Southern
Decorative Arts
924 South Main Street
Winston-Salem, N.C. 27101
Fifteen period rooms, with
furniture and objects of the
South from 1600 to 1820.

Old Salem
Old Salem Road/Drawer F
Salem Station
Winston-Salem, N.C. 27108
(919)723–3688
Restored 18th- and 19th-
century Moravian town with
8 exhibit buildings, house-
museums with period
furnishings, and craft
demonstrations.

Tennessee
Great Smoky Mountain
National Park
Gatlinburg, Tenn. 37738
(615)436–5615
One hundred 18th- to
early 20th-century log-
cabin structures, with pioneer
museum and mill
demonstrations.

The Hermitage
Rachels Lane
Hermitage, Tenn. 37076
(615)889–2941
Historic house of 1835 with
family furnishings, situated
on 625 acres with flower
gardens.

Center for Southern
Folklore
1216 Peabody Avenue
Memphis, Tenn. 38104
(901)726–4205
Artifacts, contemporary folk
art, and crafts from the
20th-century South.

Fort Nashborough
170 First Avenue North
Nashville, Tenn. 37201
(615)255–8192
Five buildings and log
replica of the first
settlement of 1779, with
implements, furnishings, and
craft demonstrations.

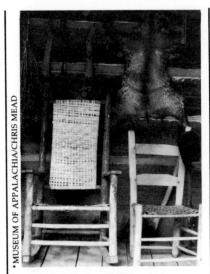

Museum of Appalachia*
Box 359/Highway 61
Norris, Tenn. 37828
(615)482–3481
Thirteen reconstructed and
furnished log cabins,
including a
blacksmith shop,
corn-grinding mill,
smokehouse,
broom and rope
factory, and display barn
with frontier and pioneer
memorabilia.

Virginia
Kenmore
1201 Washington Avenue
Fredericksburg, Va. 22401
(703)373–3381
Home of
George Washington's
sister, built in 1752, with
18th-century furnishings,
18th-century working
kitchen, and museum
building with exhibits.

Mary Washington House
1200 Charles Street
Fredericksburg, Va. 22401
(703)373–1569
George Washington's
mother's house,
built in 1772,
with period furnishings.

Jamestown Festival Park
Glass House Point
Jamestown, Va. 23081
Mail: Box JF
Williamsburg,
Va. 23185
Reconstruction of 17th-
century James Fort and its
buildings, and Powhatan's
lodge.

Jamestown Island
Jamestown, Va. 23081
(804)898–3400
Interpretation of first
permanent
English settlement
in New World of 1607.

Mount Vernon
Mount Vernon, Va. 22121
(703)780–2000
Historic house of George
Washington; exhibits include
family furniture, paintings,
a greenhouse, and garden.

Colonial Williamsburg*
P.O. Box C
Williamsburg, Va. 23185
(804)229–1000
Re-created 18th-century
colonial town, including
shops, houses, public
buildings, and gardens.

West Virginia
Harpers Ferry National
Historical Park
Harpers Ferry, W. Va. 25425
(304)535–6371
Nineteenth-century restored
historic "old business
district" of Harpers Ferry.

MIDWEST AND WEST

Arizona
Pioneer Arizona
Interstate 17 at Pioneer Road
Phoenix, Ariz. 85061
(602)993–0210
Reconstruction of typical
Arizona town of late
19th century; 26 buildings.

Arkansas
Arkansas Territorial
Restoration
Third and Scott Streets
Little Rock, Ark. 72201
(501)371–2348
Four mid-19th-century
restored houses with period
furnishings; also an 1850s
log house.

Iowa
Norwegian-American Museum
502 West Water Street
Decorah, Iowa 52101
(319)382–9681
Illustrates history of early
Norwegian immigrants.
The museum complex is
divided into 3 segments:
museum building; outdoor
area with pioneer homes and
schoolhouse; and industrial
division exhibiting early
agriculture, carpentry, and
blacksmithing.

Kansas
Historic Wichita "Cowtown"
1871 Sim Park Drive
Wichita, Kans. 67203
(316)264–0671
Restoration of early pioneer
Wichita from 1860 to 1880;
26 buildings.

Michigan
Greenfield Village and
Henry Ford Museum
Dearborn, Mich. 48121
(313)271–1620

Village situated on 260
acres, with over 100 restored
buildings from all over the
United States, tracing 3
centuries of American arts
and skills, with examples of
architecture and furnishings.
Museum's exhibits include
collections of Americana in
the decorative, mechanical,
and industrial arts.

Detroit Institute of Arts
5200 Woodward Avenue
Detroit, Mich. 48202
(313)833–7900
Robert Tannahill wing:
American decorative arts,
paintings, and
sculpture from
the late 17th century
through the early 20th
century.

New Mexico
Museum of International
Folk Art
P.O. Box 2978
706 Camino Lejo
Santa Fe, N. Mex. 87503
(505)827–2544
Folk art objects from around
the world: collections include
folk costumes, majolica
(tin-glazed pottery), Spanish
colonial arts, textiles, and
Alpine art.

Old Cienega Village Museum
Route 2/Box 214
Santa Fe, N. Mex. 87501
(505)471–2261
Situated on 350 acres with
numerous buildings, among
them a 17th-century "placita"
house with Spanish colonial
furnishings, an 18th-century
house and functional
buildings, a Sierra mountain
village, depicting life in the
18th and 19th centuries, and
a reconstructed morada
"penitente meetinghouse."

Ohio

Dunham Tavern Museum
6709 Euclid Avenue
Cleveland, Ohio 44103
(216)431–1060
Historic house built in 1824,
with period furnishings.

The Massillon Museum
212 Lincoln Way East
Massillon, Ohio 44646
(216)833–4061
Changing collections of
American folk art exhibited
in historic 1835 house.

Schoenbrunn Village
Box 129
New Philadelphia,
Ohio 44663
(216)339–3636
Re-created late 18th-century
Indian village with 19 log
structures, burial grounds,
school, and church.

The Shaker Historical
Society Museum
16740 South Park Boulevard
Shaker Heights, Ohio 44120
(216)921–1201
Collections of 19th-century
Shaker furniture of the North
Union Colony and eastern
communities.

Oregon

Aurora Colony
Historical Society
Second and Liberty Streets
Aurora, Oreg. 97002
(503)678–5754
Maintains 3 historic dwellings:
Ox Barn Museum, Kraus
House, and Steinbach Cabin;
associated with the Aurora
Colony, a communal society
founded in 1856.

Robert Newell House
8089 Champoeg Road N.E.
Champoeg, Oreg. 97137
(503)678–5537

Reconstructed residence of
1852, with authentic furniture
from Oregon's pioneers and
exhibits including pioneer
quilts and Indian baskets.

Pioneer Mother's
Memorial Cabin
8035 Champoeg Road N.E.
Champoeg, Oreg. 97137
(503)633–2237
Cabin of hand-hewn logs
with shake roof, furnished
with pioneer items.

Dr. Henry John
Minthorn House
115 South River Street
Molalla, Oreg. 97038
(503)538–2831
Pioneer Quaker house, where
President Herbert Hoover
grew up; house belonged
to his uncle.

Mission Mill Museum
Mill Street
Salem, Oreg. 97301
(503)364–4019 or
(503)585–7012
Includes several mid-
19th-century buildings:
Jason Lee House, Methodist
Mission Parsonage,
John D. Boon House,
Mission, and Thomas Kay
Woolen Mill buildings.

*HENKEL SQUARE/CHRIS MEAD

*BAYOU BEND/CHRIS MEAD

Texas

Bayou Bend Collection of
Museum of Fine Arts *
1 Westcott Street/Box 13157
Houston, Tex. 77019
(713)529–8773
Twenty-two rooms of
American decorative arts
from the 17th to 19th
centuries.

Henkel Square Restoration *
P.O. Box 82
Round Top, Tex. 78954
(713)622–4889
Authentic representation of
life of early German settlers
in Texas, includes pre-Civil
War houses with furnishings.

Winedale Historical Center
of the University of Texas
at Austin
P.O. Box 11
Round Top, Tex. 78954
(713)278–3530
Center for the study of the
ethnic cultures of central
Texas, consisting of 190-acre
farmstead with
original house
and outbuildings and 3
additional pre-Civil War
buildings.

Washington

Fort Vancouver National
Historic Site
Vancouver, Wash. 98660
(206)696–7655
Partial reconstruction of
important farming and
manufacturing community,
and fur trade capital, with
stockade and buildings as
they appeared during the
1840s.

Wisconsin

Stonefield
Cassville, Wis. 53806
(608)725–5210
Agricultural museum with
1890s replica of pioneer
village and 19th-century
Nelson Dewey House and
grounds.

Milton House
16 South Janesville
Milton, Wis. 53563
(608)868–7772
Restored inn of 1844, with
collections of Indian and
pioneer relics, and 1837 log
cabin.

252

Directory of Antiques Dealers

The *Directory of Antiques Dealers* lists 541 dealers throughout the United States who specialize in American Country antiques. Many dealers do business only by appointment, so it is advisable to call before you visit. In addition to individual locations, there are also antiques shows at which groups of dealers offer a large and varied collection of pieces. Renninger's in Kutztown, Pa., has a particularly fine show every weekend, and prices are very reasonable. Because there is no central agency that lists dates and locations of antiques shows, the best way to find out about these events is through local dealers in the area you are visiting.

ALABAMA

Chandler and Cooper Antiques
114 Gin Street
Springville, Ala. 35146
(205)467–6371

ARIZONA

Arcadia Studio
3940 East Campbell Avenue
Phoenix, Ariz. 85018
(602)956–3950

J. H. Armer Company
6926 Main Street
Scottsdale, Ariz. 85251
(602)947–2407

Bishop Gallery
7164 Main Street
Scottsdale, Ariz. 85251
(602)949–9062

Antiques America
123 South Eastbourne—
#16 Broadway Village
Tucson, Ariz. 85716
(602)327–8697

Just Us On Court
299 North Court Avenue
Tucson, Ariz. 85701
(602)622–3607

CALIFORNIA

The Snow Goose Antiques
1010 Torrey Pines Road
La Jolla, Calif. 92037
(714)454–4893

Peace and Plenty
P.O. Box 27367
Los Angeles, Calif. 90027
(213)462–5282

★ WHITELEY/CHRIS MEAD

L. D. Whiteley Galleries of American Folk Art ★
303 North Sweetzer
Los Angeles, Calif. 90048
(213)658–8820

Williamsburg West Antiques
140 West Main Street
Los Gatos, Calif. 95030
(408)354–3332

Drury Lane Antiques
512 West Chapman Avenue
Orange, Calif. 92668
(714)997–2384

Jean Warden Antiques
1617 North Garey Avenue
Pomona, Calif. 91767
(714)623–4518

Kiracofe and Kile
955 Fourteenth Street
San Francisco, Calif. 94114
(415)431–1222

The Three Witches Antiques
2843 California Street
San Francisco, Calif. 94115
(415)922–0940

Tin Duck Antiques
3018 Goldsmith Street
Santa Monica, Calif. 90405
(213)396–5626

The Blue Candlestick Antiques
20375 Saratoga—
Los Gatos Road
Saratoga, Calif. 95070
(408)867–3658

Adams House
137 West First Street
Tustin, Calif. 92680
(714)838–0742

Tin Duck Antiques
1329 West Washington Boulevard
Venice, Calif. 90291
(213)396–3644

COLORADO

Bishop Gallery
South St. Vrain Highway
Allenspark, Colo. 80510
(303)747–2419

CONNECTICUT

Jerard Paul Jordan Gallery
P.O. Box 71/Slade Acres
Ashford, Conn. 06278
(203)429–7954

Gene and Jo Sue Coppa
20 East Woodhaven Drive
Avon, Conn. 06001
(203)673–3722

Leon W. Fey Antiques
73 Paper Chase Trail
Avon, Conn. 06001
(203)673–5736

Robert Kneeland
Amity Road
Bethany, Conn. 06525
(203)387–1712

J. J. Smith
93 Bethmore Road
Bethany, Conn. 06525
(203)543–9943

Crass & Graf
158 Greenwood Ave.
Bethel, Conn. 06801
(203)748–8039

Ed Clerk Antiques
RD 1/Box 223
Bethlehem, Conn. 06751
(203)567–5093

Ravenwood Antiques
Route 1/Box 297
Hickory Lane
Bethlehem, Conn. 06751
(203)266–7050

Hailston House Antiques
Route 85/59 West Street
Bolton, Conn. 06040
(203)646–2877

Ray Cox
Essex Square
Essex, Conn. 06426
(203)767–2270 Shop
(203)767–8704 Home

Robert Spencer
Essex Square
Essex, Conn. 06426
(203)767–8655

Patty Gagarin Antiques
Banks North Road
Fairfield, Conn. 06430
(203)259–7332

Manya Piels
208 South Benson Road
Fairfield, Conn. 06430
(203)255–6242

David A. Schorsch
313 Stanwich Road
Greenwich, Conn. 06830
(203)869–5310

Ginger English Antiques
Main Street
Kent, Conn. 06757
(203)927–4428

Lewis W. Scranton Antiques
Roast Meat Hill
Killingworth, Conn. 06417
(203)663–1060

Jerome Blum
Willow Corners Antiques
Ross Hill Road
Lisbon, Conn. 06351
(203)376–0300

Litchfield Hills Antiques
On-The-Green
Litchfield, Conn. 06759
(203)567–8607

Kathryn and Fred Giampietro
3210 Whitney Avenue
Mount Carmel, Conn. 06514
(203)787–3851

Joseph Pari
3846 Whitney Avenue
Mount Carmel/Hamden,
Conn. 06518
(203)248–4951

Carolyn Buckingham
New Canaan, Conn.
(203)966–1035

Kathy Schoemer*
New Canaan, Conn.
(203)966–0841

Cod Fish Antiques
P.O. Box 361
Newtown, Conn. 06470
(203)426–6055

Thomas Gray Antiques
Hewitt Road
North Stonington,
Conn. 06359
(203)535–0637

Falcon Antiques
184 Main Street
Old Wethersfield, Conn.
06109
(203)529–7262

Darien Reece
Great Pasture Road
Redding, Conn. 06875
(203)938–9366

Suzanne Kristoff
113 West Lane
Ridgefield, Conn. 06877
(203)438–8931

Silver Spring Farm
Judy Lenett
Ridgefield, Conn. 06877
(203)438–7713

Devotion House Antiques
Route 97
Scotland, Conn. 06264
(203)456–0452

John and Jan Davidson
96 East Weatogue Street
Simsbury, Conn. 06070
(203)658–6525

Foster and Lanergan
Antiques
56 County Road
Simsbury, Conn. 06070
(203)658–9841

J. B. Richardson Gallery
362 Pequot Avenue
Southport, Conn. 06490
(203)259–1903
(203)226–0358

Joan Huntington
Woodlot Antiques
Cedar Road
Southport, Conn. 06490
(203)259–7173

Marguerite Riordan
8 Pearl Street
Stonington, Conn. 06378
(203)535–2511

Shirley E. Fantone, Antiques
175 Simsbury Road
West Granby, Conn. 06090
(203)653–6411

Blackmar Antiques
224 Danbury Road
Wilton, Conn. 06897
(203)762–8717

Mead Tavern Antiques
2 De Forest Road
Wilton, Conn. 06897
(203)762–5317
(203)762–5753

Lincoln Sander
270 Cannon Road
Wilton, Conn. 06897
(203)762–3265

Kenneth Hammitt, Inc.
S. Main Street
Woodbury, Conn. 06798
(203)263–5676

Sheila Rideout
128 Minortown Road
Woodbury, Conn. 06798
(203)263–4239

Robert S. Walin Antiques
547 Flanders Road
Woodbury, Conn. 06798
(203)263–4416

Moira Wallace Antiques
857 North Main Street
Woodbury, Conn. 06798
(203)263–2582

DELAWARE

Sally Borton
Shop Location:
Kennett Pike/Route 52
Fairville, Pa.
(215)388–7687
Mailing Address:
P.O. Box 3944
Greenville, Del. 19807
(302)655–4924

Paris N. Walters
Box 365
Newark, Del. 19711
(302)737–5853

Iron Age Antiques
Central Avenue and
Daisy Street
Ocean View, Del. 19970
(302)539–5344

254

The Hudson House
Benson Street and Route 1
Rehoboth Beach, Del. 19971
(302)227–2487

FLORIDA

Circa Antiques/
Juanita Grundin
1219 East Las Olas Boulevard
Fort Lauderdale, Fla. 33301
(305)462–1704

Maze Pottinger
1160 North Federal Highway
Fort Lauderdale, Fla. 33304
(305)463–4518

Brian Riba
112 Worth Court South
West Palm Beach, Fla. 33405
(305)832–6737

ILLINOIS

Golden Eagle Antiques
The Cunningham's
Rural Route 1
Arcola, Ill. 61910
(217)268–4894

Pheasant Hill Antiques
9957 Grange Hall Road
Belvidere, Ill. 61008
(815)547–6793

Apple Barn Antiques
2526 Rock Springs Road
Decatur, Ill. 62500
(217)422–1784

Shirley McGill Antiques
717 East State Street
Geneva, Ill. 60134
(312)232–4196

Cape Cod House Antiques
474 Forest Street
Glen Ellyn, Ill. 60137
(312)858–2170
(312)469–1559

*POLLACK/CHRIS MEAD

Barbara and Frank Pollack*
1303 Lincoln Avenue South
Highland Park, Ill. 60035
(312)433–2213

Puffabelly Station
Route 136 (I–55)
McLean, Ill. 61754
(309)874–2112

Town and Country Antiques
and
Ed and Fred's Antiques
407 Main Street
Mahomet, Ill. 61853
(217)356–1452

Bonnie's Bygones
530 White Oak Drive
Naperville, Ill. 60540
(312)355–2863

St. James Antiques
163 South Oak Park Avenue
Oak Park, Ill. 60302
(312)386–5319

The Trading Post
401 North East Street
Olney, Ill. 62450
(618)395–4491

Barbara A. Johnson Antiques
Clock Tower Inn—Henricis
7801 East State Street
Rockford, Ill. 61125
(815)397–6699

The Eagles Nest
7080 Old River Road
Rockford, Ill. 61105
(815)633–8410

House of Seven Fables
300 East Dale Street
Somonauk, Ill. 60552
(815)498–2289

Eastnor Gallery of Antiques
700 East Miller
Springfield, Ill. 62700
(217)523–0998
(217)787–7729

Bonnie's Carriage House
U.S. 54
Summer Hill, Ill. 62372
(217)285–4557

Marianne Clark Antiques
10817 Route 176
Woodstock, Ill. 60098
(815)459–7524

INDIANA

The Log House
20033 C. R. 16
Bristol, Ind. 46507
(219)522–3482

The Mare's Nest
U.S. 40 West/Route 1/Box 549
Cambridge, Ind. 47327
(317)478–5941

Alcorn's Antiques
214 West Main Street
Centerville, Ind. 47330
(317)855–3161

Douglas & Jacqueline
Eichhorn
208 West Main Street
Centerville, Ind. 47330
(317)855–3398

Bowie's Antiques
Route 9/Squawbuck Road
Columbia City, Ind. 46725
(219)244–3636

The Wood & Stone Antiques
1116 Pearl Street
Columbus, Ind. 47201
(812)376–8337

Country Airs Antiques
Quimby Village
1802 Bluffton Road
Fort Wayne, Ind. 46809
(219)747–4705

Pottinger—Walters Antiques
108 North Main Street
Goshen, Ind. 46526
(219)533–9416

Cellar House
Huntington, Ind.
(219)356–7072

Ewing's Antiques
7718 North Michigan Road
Indianapolis, Ind. 46268
(317)299–6074
(317)257–6943

Folkways Antiques
1404 North New Jersey Street
Indianapolis, Ind. 46202
(317)634–8085

Red Barn Antiques
325 East 106 Street
Indianapolis, Ind. 46280
(317)846–8929

Bette Ann Antiques
415 Fourth Avenue
Jonesboro, Ind. 46938
(317)674–1654

Jay & Ellen Carter Antiques
State Road 135 North
Nashville, Ind. 47448
(812)988–7904

Country Cottage Antiques
505 West Jennings
Newburgh, Ind. 47630
(812)853–7938

Two Lady Antiques
505 West Main
Newburgh, Ind. 47630
(812)853–9110

255

Charles Dickens House
Antiques
Main Street/Highway 13
North Webster, Ind. 46555
(219)834–7252

Betsy Ross House Antiques
Main Street/Highway 13
North Webster, Ind. 46555
(219)834–7252

Bittersweet Farm Antiques
Box 24
Stamford, Ind. 47463
(812)825–9943

Dovetail Antiques
101 Dewey Avenue
Washington, Ind. 47501
(812)254–7622

Jane and Henry Eckert
Antiques
131 West Main
Westfield, Ind. 46074
(317)896–3081

KENTUCKY

Sapp Brothers Antiques
East Broadway/Highway 208
Campbellsville, Ky. 42718
(502)789–1497

Finders Keepers Antiques
115 East Main Street
Flemingsburg, Ky. 41041
(606)759–7738

Precious Memories Antiques
629 Clayton Avenue
Georgetown, Ky. 40324
(502)863–3606

Americana Antiques
Rural Route 4
Lancaster, Ky. 40444
(606)548–3681

Country Village Antiques
Lancaster, Ky.
(606)548–4291
(606)792–3133

Woodford Landing Antiques
185 South Main
Versailles, Ky. 40383
(606)873–6505 Shop
(606)873–8400 Home

MAINE

Barbara Thornsjo
Cock Hill Farm
Bessey Ridge Road
Albion, Maine 04910
(207)437–2345

Creative Antiques
Route 175
Brooklin, Maine 04616
(207)359–8525

Country Cousin Antiques
25 Central Street
Camden, Maine 04843
(207)236–4153

Rufus Foshee Antiques
Route 1/P.O. Box 531
Camden, Maine 04843
(207)236–2838

W. J. French Antiques
10 High Street
Camden, Maine 04843
(207)236–3807

Hanson's Carriage House
Two Lights and Ocean House
Roads
Cape Elizabeth, Maine 04107
(207)767–3608

Pillsbury's Antiques
Two Lights Road
Cape Elizabeth, Maine 04107
(207)799–0638

Cranberry Hill Antiques
and Lighting
Route 1
Cape Neddick, Maine 03902
(207)363–5178

Wind Mill Antiques
State Street
Castine, Maine 04421
(207)326–8819

Patricia Anne Reed
Bristol Road/Route 130
Damariscotta, Maine 04543
(207)563–5633

Bell and Kettle Antiques
Routes 113 and 5
East Brownfield, Maine 04010
(207)935–3182

Maple Avenue Antiques
23 Maple Avenue
Farmington, Maine 04938
(207)778–4850

Berdan's
151 Water Street
Hallowell, Maine 04347
(207)622–0151

Barbara Thornsjo
128 Water Street
Hallowell, Maine 04347
(207)437–2345

Hermitage Antiques
Edes Falls Road
Harrison, Maine 04040
(207)583–2821

Bunker Hill Antiques
Shop Location:
Route 213
Jefferson, Maine 04847
Mailing Address:
Box 349
Newcastle, Maine 04553
(207)563–3167

The Chapman House Antiques
Beach Street/Box 647
Kennebunkport, Maine 04046
(207)967–3005

Post Road Association
Coastal Route 1
Kittery, Maine 03904
(207)439–0578

Kenneth and Ida Manko
P.O. Box 20
Moody Point, Maine 04054
(207)646–2595

Jack Partridge Antiques
Route 1
North Edgecomb,
Maine 04556
(207)882–7745

David and Nan Gurley
Shop Location:
Route 160
North Parsonsfield, Maine
Mailing Address:
Kezar Falls, Maine 04047
(207)625–3577

Phipps of Pittston
Shop Location:
Route 27
Pittston, Maine 04345
Mailing Address:
P.O. Box 841
Gardiner, Maine 04345
(207)582–3555

Barridoff Galleries
242 Middle Street
Portland, Maine 04104
(207)772–5011

Hanson's Carriage House
130 Park Street
Portland, Maine 04101
(207)774–0187

Paul L. Ackerman
23 Main Street
Rockport, Maine 04856
(207)236–4832

Town Shop Antiques
Seaport Drive
Rockport, Maine 04856
(207)236–8280

Pumpkin Patch
Route 1
Searsport, Maine 04974
(207)548–6047

Auld Lang Syne Antiques
Route 202
South China, Maine 04358
(207)445–2245

The Ebenezer Alden House
Antiques
Union, Maine 04862
(207)785–2881

MacDougall—Gionet Antiques
Route 1/Box 278/RFD 2
Wells, Maine 04090
(207)646–3531

1685 Mill House
Box 193/Route 1
Wells, Maine 04090
(207)646–9444

Cavanaugh Gallery of Art
and Antiques
Custom House
Main Street/Route 1–A
Winterport, Maine 04496
(207)223–4314

The Coach House
Pleasant Street
Wiscasset, Maine 04578
(207)882–7833

Drury and Rice Early New
England Antiques
Shop Location:
Route 1
Woolwich, Maine 04579
Mailing Address:
RFD 3/Box 206
Wiscasset, Maine 04578
(207)443–6526

Pamela Cushman
21 Portland Street
Yarmouth, Maine 04096
(207)846–9038

Roberta Hansen
Prince's Point
Yarmouth, Maine 04096
(207)846–4926

MARYLAND

"All of Us Americans,"
Folk Art
Bettie Mintz
P.O. Box 5943
Bethesda, Md. 20014
(301)652–4626

Gary A. Boyd
4857 Battery Lane
Bethesda, Md. 20014
(301)652–0123

Stella Rubin
Query Mill Road
Gaithersburg, Md. 20760
(301)948–4187

Frederick B. Hanson
Pry Mill
Box 35/RD 1
Keedysville, Md. 21756
(301)797–3895

Comus Antiques
North Federal Street
New Market, Md. 21774
(301)831–6464

The Klackers,
Wallace and Letitia
108 West Main Street
New Market, Md. 21774
(301)865–5324

Jerry E. Tiller
Route 1/Box 55
Pocomoke, Md. 21851
(301)957–0429

Norma and William Wangel
11058 Seven Hill Lane
Potomac, Md. 20854
(301)299–8430

The Willow Tree
11905 Devilwood Drive
Potomac, Md. 20854
(301)762–3748

MASSACHUSETTS

Hidden River Antiques
Shop Location:
Bellus Road
Ashfield, Mass. 01330
Mailing Address:
RFD 1
Shelburne Falls, Mass. 01370
(413)625–9328

Sprig of Thyme Antiques
Box 128
Ashfield, Mass. 01330
(413)628–4491

Ruth Gordon Ellis Antiques
East Main Street
Ashley Falls, Mass. 01222
(413)229–7947

Marge's Nook Antiques
284 South Main St./
Routes 202 and 2–A
Athol, Mass. 01331
(617)249–7488

Sage House Antiques
Route 23/On the Common
Blandford, Mass. 01008
(413)848–2843

Keepsake House
Shop Location:
Route 6–A
Brewster, Mass. 02631
Mailing Address:
Box 1016
Orleans, Mass. 02653
(617)255–5036
(617)432–0851

Brimfield Antiques
Susan and Richard Raymond
Main Street
Brimfield, Mass. 01010
(413)245–3350

Cheshire Village Antiques
Route 8
Cheshire, Mass. 01225
(413)743–4385

Conway House
Route 116
Conway, Mass. 01341
(413)369–4660

Stephen Score
159 Main Street
Essex, Mass. 01929
(617)768–6252

Grain Mill Antiques
Depot Avenue
Falmouth, Mass. 02540
(617)548–0241

The Herb Farm
Barnard Road
Granville, Mass. 01034
(413)357–8882

Paul and Susan Kleinwald
"The Curious Collector"
252 Main Street/Route 7
Great Barrington,
Mass. 01230
(413)528–4252

Down Home
173 Main Street/Route 7
Great Barrington,
Mass. 01230
(413)528–0544

Great Bridge Antiques
105 Main Street/Route 7
Great Barrington,
Mass. 01230
(413)528–2643

Pam Boynton
Pleasant Street
Groton, Mass. 01450
(617)448–5031

The Windle Shoppe
Ridge Road
Hardwick, Mass. 01037
(413)477–8714

Penelope W. Princi
Penelope's Primitives
P.O. Box 8
Hyannis Port, Mass. 02647
(617)775–8844

257

Amber Springs Antiques
South Main Street/Route 7
Lanesborough, Mass. 01237
(413)442–1237

Pinewood Shop
Route 102
Lee, Mass. 01238
(413)243–0905

Charles L. Flint
81 Church Street/Box 88
Lenox, Mass. 01240
(413)637–1634 Shop
(413)637–0583 Gallery
(413)243–9835 Home

Charles L. Flint Antiques and
Lyman Galleries (Antique Art)
69 Church Street/Box 88
Lenox, Mass. 01240
(413)637–1634 Shop
(413)637–0583 Gallery
(413)243–9835 Home

Veronica Harrington Antiques
67 Church Street
Lenox, Mass. 01240
(413)637–0587

Sherri James Antiques
17 Housatonic Street
Lenox, Mass. 01240
(413)637–1212
(413)637–3356

South River Primitives
22 Main Street
Route 3–A at 139
Marshfield, Mass. 02050
(617)834–7774

Paul Madden Antiques
5 North Water Street
Nantucket, Mass. 02554
(617)228–0112

Tranquil Corners Antiques
38 Center Street
Nantucket, Mass. 02554
(617)228–0848

Toppan House Antiques
Route 1–A/5 High Road
Newbury, Mass. 01950
(617)462–6353

Leonard's Antiques, Inc.
600 Taunton Avenue
Route 44
Seekonk, Mass. 02771
(617)336–8585

Dovetail Antiques
North Main Street/Route 7
Sheffield, Mass. 01257
(413)229–2628

Lawrence Goldsmith
South Main Street
Sheffield, Mass. 01257
(413)229–6660

Bird Cage Antiques
Main Street/Route 23
South Egremont, Mass. 01258
(413)528–3556
(413)528–9049

Ardenbrug Antiques
Route 102
South Lee, Mass. 01238
(413)243–3471
(413)243–0001

Riverrun Antiques
Route 102
South Lee, Mass. 01238
(413)243–2142

G and S Antiques
"North Meadow"
Sunderland, Mass. 01375
(413)665–2920

Country Interiors
402 Washington Street
Wellesley Hills, Mass. 02181
(617)237–9340

1843 House Antiques
Corner Christian Lane and
Routes 5 and 10
Whately, Mass. 01093
(413)665–3239

The Victorian Shop
610 Main Street
Williamstown, Mass. 01267
(413)458–3037

MICHIGAN

Leonard Berry—Gordon
Greek Antiques
726 North Woodward Avenue
Birmingham, Mich. 48011
(313)646–1996

Amariah Antiques
Amariah Prouty House
302 Elm Street
Kalamazoo, Mich. 49007
(616)345–4474

Robert and Cynthia Baker
P.O. Box 32
Niles, Mich. 49120
(616)683–4545

Timothy and Pamela Hill
56000 Ten Mile Road
South Lyon, Mich. 48178
(313)437–1538

MINNESOTA

Robert J. Riesberg
343 Salem Church Road
Saint Paul, Minn. 55118
(612)457–1772

MISSISSIPPI

7 C's Antiques
103 North Lamar Street
Oxford, Miss. 38655
(601)234–2088

MISSOURI

Patchwork Sampler
9735 Clayton Rd.
St. Louis, MO 63124
(314)997-6116

NEW HAMPSHIRE

Amherst Village Antiques
Boston Post Road
Amherst, N.H. 03031
(603)673–5946

The Carriage Shed Antiques
Route 101/Walnut Hill Road
Amherst, N.H. 03031
(603)673–2944

Theresa and Arthur Greenblatt
P.O. Box 276
Amherst, N.H. 03031
(603)673–4401

Halverson's Antiques
Route 101
Amherst, N.H. 03031
(603)673–2752

Fern Rock Antiques
Main Street
Ashland, N.H. 03217
(603)968–7030

Bell Hill Antiques
Route 101 and Bell Hill
Road—Houck Realty Building
Bedford, N.H. 03102
(603)472–5580

Old Chester Antiques
Raymond Road
Chester, N.H. 03036
(603)887–4778

Fred and Joanne Cadarette
Shop Location:
Route 129 East
Concord, N.H.
Mailing Address:
RFD 2
Pittsfield, N.H. 03263
(603)435–6615

The Rooster Antiques
RFD 4
Concord, N.H. 03301
(603)798–5912

Doug and Elizabeth Kingsley
Maple Street/Route 127
Contoocook, N.H. 03229
(603)746–4442

Lewis and Fortier Antiques
Maple Street/Route 127
Contoocook, N.H. 03229
(603)746–3078

1680 House Antiques
Route 108
East Kingston, N.H. 03827
(603)642–3153

258

The Arthurs' Antiques
Rural Route 1
Epsom, N.H. 03234
(603)736–4739

October Stone Antiques
Jady Hill
Exeter, N.H. 03833
(603)772–2024

William Lewan Antiques
Old Troy Road
Fitzwilliam, N.H. 03447
(603)585–3365

The Cobbs
Old Dublin Road
Hancock, N.H. 03449
(603)525–4053

Hardings of Hancock
Depot Street
Hancock, N.H. 03449
(603)525–3518

*PINE CONE ANTIQUES/CHRIS MEAD

Pine Cone Antiques*
Dartmouth College Highway/
Route 10 on the Common
Haverhill, N.H. 03765
(603)989–5983

Felsen's Antiques
Main Street
Henniker, N.H. 03242
(603)428–7512

Well Sweep Antiques
Hillsboro Centre, N.H. 03244
(603)464–3218

Stanley A. & Clara Jean Davis
The Old Parsonage
Shop Location:
Routes 202 and 9
Hopkinton, N.H.
Mailing Address:
RFD 1
Concord, N.H. 03301
(603)228–0217

MacGregor's Barn
Route 103
Hopkinton, N.H. 03301
(603)746–3862

Mitchell's Antiques
Shop Location:
Rollins Road
Hopkinton, N.H.
Mailing Address:
RFD 1
Concord, N.H. 03301
(603)746–5056

Beech Hill Gallery
Old Concord Road
Keene, N.H. 03431
(603)352–2194

Dale Pregent Antiques
142 Marlboro Street
Keene, N.H. 03431
(603)352–6736

Brick House Antiques
McKinley Circle
Marlborough, N.H. 03455
(603)876–3765

Thomas R. Longacre–Antiques
Route 124
Marlborough, N.H. 03455
(603)876–4080

Betty Willis Antiques
Jaffrey Road
Marlborough, N.H. 03455
(603)876–3983

Burlwood Antique Shop
Route 3
Meredith, N.H. 03253
(603)279–6387

Virginia Aceti and Sheryl
Duquette
Pioneer Homestead
Appleton Road/RFD 1/
Box 438
New Ipswich, N.H. 03071
(603)878–2622

Peter H. Eaton Antiques, Inc.
Thornell Road
Newton Junction, N.H. 03859
(603)382–6838

Joan's Antiques
At the Common
Plaistow, N.H. 03865
(603)382–5000

R. Leonard and Company
Antiques
111 Main Street/Route 121–A
Plaistow, N.H. 03865
(603)382–8912

Margaret Scott Carter, Inc.
175 Market Street
Portsmouth, N.H. 03801
(603)436–1781

Strafford Corner Antiques
293 Pond Hill Road
Rochester, N.H. 03867
(603)332–4264

Old Town Farm Antiques
Old Town Farm Road/Box 278
South Peterborough, N.H.03458
(603)924–3523

Harrison House Antiques
Shop Location:
Route 77
South Weare, N.H.
Mailing Address:
Rural Route 1/Box 384
South Weare, N.H. 03281
(603)529–7174

Arthur W. Abbott Antiques
Sanborn Road
Tilton, N.H. 03276
(603)286–8230

Knollcroft Antiques
Hillsboro
Upper Village, N.H. 03244
(603)478–5771

Mary Page Antiques
Burnt Hill Road
Warner, N.H. 03278
(603)456–3351

Tintagel Antiques
Route 31
Washington, N.H. 03280
(603)495–3429

Elizabeth Stokes Antiques
Sugar Hill Road South
Weare, N.H. 03281
(603)529–2363

Campton Antiques
Route 3
West Campton, N.H. 03228
(603)726–7054

NEW JERSEY

The White House
215 Myrtle Avenue/Route 202
Boonton, N.J.
(201)335–4926
(201)839–7258

Emanon Corner Antiques
Rural Route 1/Box 338
Califon, N.J. 07830
(201)832–7892

259

Antiques at Copan Meeting
RD 2/Box 265
Columbus. N.J. 08022
(609)261–2733

Leonard Balish
P.O. Box 25/124A Engle
Street
Englewood, N.J. 07631
(201)568–5385

Henry B. Holt
18 Oval Road
Essex Fells, N.J. 07021
(201)228–0853

Pewter and Pine Shop
Franklin Lakes, N.J. 07417
(201)891–3626

Bogwater Jim Antiques
Route 15
Lafayette, N.J. 07848
(201)383–8170

Anthony and Ellen Barrett
Antiques
South Main Street
Mullica Hill, N.J. 08062
(609)478–4120

Robert and Ann Schumann
74 North Main Street
Mullica Hill, N.J. 08062
(609)478–2553

Tewksbury Antiques
The Crossroads
Oldwick, N.J. 08858
(201)439–2221

Janet and Elliot Greene
47 Old Forge Road
Ringwood, N.J. 07457
(201)666–3346

Catherine Blair Antiques
350 Springfield Avenue
Summit, N.J. 07901
(201)273–5771

Betty Klein—Country
Primitive Furniture and
Accessories
Tenafly, N.J. 07670
(201)567–1664

Cedar House Antiques
Oceanview Drive
Toms River, N.J. 08753
(201)929–0573

NEW MEXICO

Dewey—Kofron Gallery
112 East Palace Avenue
Santa Fe, N. Mex. 87501
(505)982–8632
(505)982–8478

Habitat
222 Shelby
Santa Fe, N. Mex. 87501
(505)982–3722
(505)983–5463

NEW YORK

Suzanne Courcier and
Robert Wilkins
Star Route/Route 22
Austerlitz, N.Y. 12017
(518)392–5754

Union Valley Antiques
RD 1/Box 133
Bainbridge, N.Y. 13733
(607)967–8262

Oxen Hill Antiques
35 Andrews Avenue
Binghamton, N.Y. 13904
(607)723–0841

The Back Barn Antiques
P.O. Box 1080
Montauk Highway
Bridgehampton, N.Y. 11932
(516)324–2112
(516)536–0821

Bird in Hand Antiques
Main Street
Bridgehampton, N.Y. 11932
(516)537–3838

Judy Corman
Main Street
Bridgehampton, N.Y. 11932
(516)537–3554

Country Cupboard Antiques
Montauk Highway and
Hayground Road
Bridgehampton, N.Y. 11932
(516)728–6516

Hayground Antiques
Montauk Highway and
Hayground Road
Bridgehampton, N.Y. 11932
(516)537–0578

Pine Cupboard Antiques
Main Street/Box 577
Bridgehampton, N.Y. 11932
(516)537–3868

The Quilt Gallery
Main Street
Bridgehampton, N.Y. 11932
(516)725–2344

Sterling and Hunt
Box 300
Bridgehampton, N.Y. 11932
(516)537–1096

Samuel Herrup Antiques
11 Dean Street
Brooklyn, N.Y. 11201
(212)875–5295

Leslie Eisenberg Antiques
820 Madison Avenue
New York, N.Y. 10021
(212)628-5454

Pineapple Primitives, Inc.
35 Pineapple Street
Brooklyn Heights, N.Y. 11201
(212)596–3342

Mother Lode
Company Antiques
Charlotte Valley
Charlottesville, N.Y. 12036
(607)397–8856

Greenwillow Farm Ltd.
Raup Road
Chatham, N.Y. 12037
(518)392–9654

Brad del Sorbo
RD/Box 235A
South Cross Road
Chatham, N.Y. 12037
(518)392–3542

The Iron Eagle
Willard Road
Chenango Forks, N.Y. 13746
(607)648–3426

Marilyn Quigley's
Lamplighter Antiques
136 Main Street
Chester, N.Y. 10918
(914)469–2654

Stone Hedge Antiques
Shop Location:
Route 236
Claverack, N.Y.
Mailing Address:
RD 4/Box 191
Hudson, N.Y. 12534
(518)851–9639

Axtell Antiques
1 River Street
Deposit, N.Y. 13754
(607)467–2353

Richard and Betty Ann Rasso
Corner Route 295
and Frisbee Street
East Chatham, N.Y. 12060
(518)392–4501

Tinn Brook Antiques
Route 52
East Walden, N.Y. 12586
(914)778–7497

Mina Trachtenberg
89 Anchorage Road
Germantown, N.Y. 12526
(518)537–6508

Marion Lewis Cobb
Scotchtown Road/RD 1
Goshen, N.Y. 10924
(914)294–7049

Hearthside Antiques
RD 1
East River Road
Greene, N.Y. 13778
(607)656–8312

Sugar Knoll Antiques
Route 12/Box 162
Greene, N.Y. 13778
(607)656–8036

The Victorian House
Route 205/RD 1/Box 168
Hartwick, N.Y. 13348
(607)293–6644

High Falls Antiques Cache
Center of High Falls
High Falls, N.Y. 12440
(914)687–9926

Roger Ketchum and
Alice Ketchum
RD 1
Holland Patent, N.Y. 13354
(315)865–4882

Antiques and Passé
Americana
The Famous Daniel Store
Route 22
Hoosick Falls, N.Y. 12090
(518)686–5889

The Pines Antiques
RD 1
Hoosick Falls, N.Y. 12090
(518)686–9810

Round Mountain
Country Antiques
West Hook Road
Hopewell Junction,
N.Y. 12533
(914)896–9351

Van Deusen House
11 Main Street
Hurley, N.Y. 12443
(914)331–8852

Nancy Winter
Main Street
Hurley, N.Y. 12443
(914)331–2746

Elliott and Grace Snyder
Box 208
Kinderhook, N.Y. 12106
(518)799–6101

Hudson Valley Antiques
7 Green Street
Kingston, N.Y. 12401
(914)331–3732

Fred J. Johnston
Main and Wall Streets
Kingston, N.Y. 12401
(914)331–3979

J and R Ferris
Box 121/Route 20
Madison, N.Y. 13402
(315)893–7006

Old Tavern Antiques
Priscilla Hutchinson Ziesmer
Route 66
Malden Bridge, N.Y. 12115
(518)766–4143

John and Jacqueline Sideli
American Decorative Arts
Route 66
Malden Bridge, N.Y. 12115
(518)766–3547

Robert Sutter
585 North Barry Avenue
Mamaroneck, N.Y. 10543
(914)698–8535 Shop
(914)948–1857 Home

Vin-Dick Antiques
RD 3/Box 117
Marbletown, N.Y. 12401
(914)338–7113

Stephen E. White Antiques
19 East Main Street
Marcellus, N.Y. 13108
(315)673–4401 Shop
(315)685–7644 Home

Kit and Caboodle Country
Antiques
RFD 3/Union School Road/
Box 248
Middletown, N.Y. 10940
(914)361–1744

Stepping Stone Inn Antiques
354 Goshen Turnpike/RD 3
Middletown, N.Y. 10940
(914)361–2261

Halfway House
219 South Plank Road/
Route 52
Newburgh, N.Y. 12550
(914)564–0589

Dan and Karen Olson
Newburgh, N.Y. 12550
(914)564–0572

Sleigh Hill Antiques
Eleanor Dill
36 Route 17K
Newburgh, N.Y. 12550
(914)562–6960

Corinne Burke
1 Forest Glen Road
New Paltz, N.Y. 12561
(914)255–1078

Thomas B. Green Antiques
6 Orchard Heights
New Paltz, N.Y. 12561
(914)255–5113

Dorothy M. Honkala
Country Charm Antiques
201 Dubois Road
New Paltz, N.Y. 12561

Sanford Levy/
Charles Glasner
Jenkinstown Antiques
520 Route 32 South
New Paltz, N.Y. 12561
(914)255–8135

Alexander Gallery
996 Madison Avenue
New York, N.Y. 10021
(212)472–1636

Marna Anderson
40 East 69th Street
New York, N.Y. 10021

Aarne Anton
12 West 18th Street/
Fifth Floor
New York, N.Y. 10011
(212)924–7146

America Hurrah Antiques
766 Madison Avenue
New York, N.Y. 10021
(212)535-1930

Mary Emmerling's American
Country Store
969 Lexington Avenue
New York, N.Y. 10021
(212)744-6705

Newman & Corwith
Bridgehampton, N.Y. 11932
(516)537-3408
By appointment

Cherchez·
864 Lexington Avenue
New York, N.Y. 10021
(212)737–8215

*CHERCHEZ/CHRIS MEAD

Davida Deutsch
New York, N.Y.
(212)586–4446

Diamant Gallery
37 West 72nd Street
New York, N.Y. 10023
(212)362–3434

Vito Giallo Antiques
966 Madison Avenue
New York, N.Y. 10021
(212)535–9885

Phyllis Haders Quilts:
Amish, Pieced, and Appliqué
New York, N.Y.
(212)832–8181

Inglenook Antiques
529 Hudson Street
New York, N.Y. 10014
(212)675–0890

Janos and Ross
110 East End Avenue/5E
New York, N.Y. 10028
(212)988–0407

Jay Johnson*
America's Folk
Heritage Gallery
1044 Madison Avenue
New York, N.Y. 10021
(212)628-7280

John Lee Kapner Antiques
100 LaSalle Street
New York, N.Y. 10027
(212)666–4999

Kelter-Malce
361 Bleecker Street
New York, N.Y. 10014
(212)989–6760

Steve Miller
American Folk Art
17 East 96th Street
New York,
N.Y. 10028
(212)348–5219

Judith and James Milne
American Country Antiques
New York, N.Y. 10028
(212)427–9642

Israel Sack, Inc.
15 East 57th Street
New York, N.Y. 10022
(212)753–6562

Pat Sales Antiques
390 Bleecker Street
New York, N.Y. 10014
(212)691–2183

George E. Schoellkopf
1065 Madison Avenue
New York, N.Y. 10028
(212)879–3672

Sanford and
Patricia Smith Gallery
19 East 76th Street
New York, N.Y. 10021
(212)929–3121

Walker Valley Antiques
100 West 94th Street/Apt. 20F
New York, N.Y. 10025
(212)866–2884

Meryl Weiss/
American Classics
300 West End Avenue
New York, N.Y. 10023
(212)787–1779

Thos. K. Woodard
American Antiques and
Quilts
835 Madison Avenue
New York, N.Y. 10021
(212)988-2906

Titicus River Antiques at
Balanced Rock
Route 116 and Keeler Lane
North Salem, N.Y. 10560
(914)669–5255

Jean Grisoni
Nyack, N.Y.
(914)358–8298

*JOHNSON/J. BARRY O'ROURKE

Old Parsonage Antiques
RD 2/Otsdawa Road
Otego, N.Y. 13825
(607)988–6390

Batterman's Antiques
10 Chenango Street
Oxford, N.Y. 13830
(607)843–2641

Cider Mill Antiques
Route 12/RD 1
Oxford, N.Y. 13830
(607)843–8985

Seeley's Antiques
37 West State Street
Oxford, N.Y. 13830
(607)843–4505

James Abbe, Jr.
45 West Main Street
Oyster Bay, N.Y. 11771
(516)922–3325
(516)921–2379

Boxwood Cottage Antiques
J. J. Pullin
RD 2/Box 110
Pine Bush, N.Y. 12566
(914)744–5285

Blue Bonnet Antiques
Route 28
Portlandville, N.Y. 13834
(607)286–7568

The Meating Place Antiques
279 Main Street
Port Washington,
N.Y. 11050
(516)883–9659

Brown and Company
P.O. Box 82/Trinity Pass
Pound Ridge,
N.Y. 10567
(914)764–8392

Mark and Marjorie Allen
RD 1/Box 10C
Putnam Valley, N.Y. 10579
(914)528–8989

262

Otto Fenn
Sag Harbor Antique Shop
P.O. Box 345
Madison Street
Sag Harbor, N.Y. 11963
(516)725–1732

A Different Drummer
20 Main Street/Route 9W
Saugerties, N.Y. 12477
(914)246–5698

Ona Curran Antiques
2336 Cayuga Road
Schenectady,
N.Y. 12309
(518)372–3653

Morgan MacWhinnie
American Country Antiques
520 North Sea Road
Southampton, N.Y. 11968
(516)283–3366

John Keith Russell Antiques
Incorporated
Spring Street
South Salem, N.Y. 10590
(914)763–3553

Clove Valley Antiques
RD 2/Box 80
Old Kings Highway
Stone Ridge, N.Y. 12484
(914)687–9795

Walker Valley Antiques
Route 52/P.O. Box 404
Walker Valley,
N.Y. 12588
(914)744–3916

Hartmann's Antiques
Hoagburg Hill Road
Box 84/RD 1
Wallkill, N.Y. 12589
(914)895–3806

Susan Martits
Corner of New Hurley and
Plains Roads
Wallkill, N.Y. 12589
(914)895–3266

Old Homestead Antiques
44 Hoagburg Hill Road
Wallkill, N.Y. 12589
(914)895–3986

Marybeth H. Keene
33 East Main Street
Waterloo, N.Y. 13165
(315)539–8195

The Sign of the Bluebird
RD 2/Unadilla Forks
West Winfield, N.Y. 13491
(315)855–4274

Joan and Larry Kindler
Antiques, Inc.
14–35 150th Street
Whitestone, N.Y. 11357
(212)767–2260

Terry Ann Tomlinson
Antiques
Box 203
Woodstock, N.Y. 12498
(914)679–6554

Frank R. Gaglio Antiques
Box 375
Wurtsboro, N.Y. 12790
(914)888–5077

NORTH CAROLINA

Elizabeth R. Daniel
2 Gooseneck Road
Chapel Hill, N.C. 27514
(919) 968–3041

The Cracker Barrel—Antiques
and Interiors
Old Highway 301
/P.O. Box 392
Elm City, N.C. 27822
(919)236–4000

Griffin's Antiques
Route 7/Box 958
Greensboro, N.C. 27407
(919)454–3362

Briar Patch Antiques
2185 Knight Road
Kernersville, N.C. 27284
(919)993–8254

Willow Oak Antiques
Route 12/Highway 52
Lexington, N.C. 27292
(919)764–0192

Ellington's Antiques
3050 Medlin Drive
Raleigh, N.C. 27607
(919)781–2383

Susan Harvey
Cullens-Baker House
Route 1/Box 93B
Tyner, N.C. 27980
(919)221–8426

The Cabin Antiques, Inc.
1438 South Stratford Road
Winston-Salem, N.C. 27103
(919)768–7659

Homestead Antiques
1403 Stratford Road/Box 1254
Winston-Salem, N.C. 27102
(919)765–6715 Home
(919)765–6813 Shop

Lindley Loy Gallery
303 Brookstown Avenue
Winston-Salem, N.C. 27101
(919)725–7284

OHIO

Darwin D. Bearley
Quilts and Country
19 Grand Avenue
Akron, Ohio 44308
(216)376–4965

Ronald Owen Dixon
415 Market Street
Brookville, Ohio 45309
(513)833–5182

The Iron Kettle
129 North Wolf Creek Street
Brookville, Ohio 45309
(513)833–2526

Timothy I. Martien
Western Reserve Antiques
14352 North Cheshire
Burton, Ohio 44021
(216)834–1577

Schmitts of Fairhaven
Rural Route 2
Camden, Ohio 45311
(513)323–4296

Edward Stvan
P.O. Box 471
Chagrin Falls, Ohio 44022
(216)247–6272

Country Wagon Antiques
427 North Street
Chardon, Ohio 44024
(216)286–3842

The Brass Bell Antiques
331 North High Street
Chillicothe, Ohio 45601
(614)773–1500

York's Olde Thing
6924 Plainfield Road
Cincinnati, Ohio 45236
(513)891–2232

Joan Jensen
Peddler Shop
9491 Taylorsville Road
Dayton, Ohio 45424
(513)233–5475

Ohio Country Furniture
2609 Stratford Road
Delaware, Ohio 43015
(614)363–1027

Drummer Boy Antiques
32 South High Street
Dublin, Ohio 43017
(614)889–2230
(614)451–9268

263

Marge Piper
Shop Location:
Fairhaven, Ohio
Mailing Address:
510 Dollar Federal Bldg.
Hamilton, Ohio 45011
(513)523–6591

🔔🔔🔔

Iron Kettle Country Antiques
106 South Maple Street
Lancaster, Ohio 43130
(614)654–3339

L. Lyle Spiess
Playhouse Antiques
362 Maple
Liberty Center, Ohio 43532
(419)533–3881

Walter Luse
Valley View Antiques
Box 197B/RD 2
Loudonville, Ohio 44842
(419)994–4716

Tin House Antiques
3341 Calumet Road
Ludlow Falls, Ohio 45339
(513)698–5595

Covered Bridge Antiques
2541 Ashland Road
Route 42N
Mansfield, Ohio 44901
(419)589–2084

The Country Peddler
Jeff and Carol Reinhard
645 West 5th Street
Marysville, Ohio 43040
(513)644–6681

Bonnie Rowlands
531 East Liberty Street
Medina, Ohio 44256
(216)725–5982

Marjorie Staufer
2244 Remsen Road
Medina, Ohio 44256
(216)239–1443

H. Alan and Nancy
Wainwright
529 South Court Street
Medina, Ohio 44256
(216)725–6249

Samaha Antiques
Public Square
Milan, Ohio 44846
(419)499–4044

Wooden Lamb
at "Stillmeadow"
Sunfish Road
Mount Gilead, Ohio 43338
(419)946–5158

Ina's Antiques
18740 Chagrin Boulevard
Shaker Heights, Ohio 44122
(216)921–8186 (Shop)
(216)238–2342 (Home)

Robert D. Leath Antiques
East Main Street
Troy, Ohio 45373
(513)335–1763

PENNSYLVANIA

Janet Schick
RD 2/Box 48
Weiler's Road
Alburtis, Pa. 18011
(215)395–5013

Antiques at 7th and Linden
48 North 7th Street
Allentown, Pa. 18101
(215)432–1494

Thomas L. Banks Antiques
Route 100
Bally, Pa. 19503
(215)845–3072

House of Antiques
2634 Old Philadelphia Pike
Bird-in-Hand, Pa. 17505
(717)394–6564

Boyertown Antiques
Weisstown and Funk Roads
Boyertown, Pa. 19512
(215)367–2452

Mike McCue Antiques
Box 158
Bryn Athyn, Pa. 19009
(215)947–4421

Edna's Antique Shoppe
General Greene Inn
Routes 263 and 413
Buckingham, Pa. 18912
(215)794–7261

Chatham Antiques
Camp Hill, Pa.
(717)737–1690

Hobby Horse Antiques
Saw Mill Road
Carversville, Pa. 18913
(215)345–7719

Yellow Barn Antiques
Box 145
Center Valley, Pa. 18034
(215)282–4965

Kenneth Lindsey Antiques
Box 232
Chadds Ford, Pa. 19317
(215)358–2160

Guthrie and Larason
Antiques
2 Butler Avenue
Route 202 at
Route 152 North
Chalfont, Pa. 18914
(215)822–3987

Robert Snyder Antiques
Limeport Pike/RD 3
Coopersburg, Pa. 18036
(215)797–8861

Stallfort Antiques
RD 1
Elverson, Pa. 19520
(215) 286–5882

Palmer and Virginia Smeltz
RD 3342/Fry Road
Fleetwood, Pa. 19522
(215)987–6129

"The Old—The Unique"
Thelma K. Tomlinson
Box 431
Forest Grove, Pa. 18922
(215)794–8317

Irvin and Dolores Boyd
Meetinghouse Antiques
509 Bethlehem Pike
Fort Washington, Pa. 19034
(215)646–5126

Franklin's Antiques
Route 263/York Road
Furlong, Pa. 18925
(215)794–8281

Durham Cabinet Shop
Route 413
Gardenville, Pa. 18926
(215)766–7104

Knorrwood Antiques
227 North Washington Street
Gettysburg, Pa. 17325
(717)642–8886

Steeley's Antiques
40 North Second Street
Hamburg, Pa. 19526
(215)562–7131

Cooper Eagle Antiques
P.O. Box 164
Huntingdon Valley, Pa. 19006
(215)947–1254
(215)675–3412

Willowdale Antiques
101 East Street Road
Kennett Square, Pa. 19348
(215)444–5377

Lilias Barger
The Lahaska Antique Courte
Lahaska, Pa. 18931
(215)794–7784

Dorothy and Abby Brooks
Lahaska Antique Courte
Route 202
Lahaska, Pa. 18931
(215)794–5461

Lippincott Antiques
Route 202
Lahaska, Pa. 18931
(215)794–7734

Jean W. Clemmer
Hickory Tree Farm
Route 113
Lederach, Pa. 19450
(215)256–6373

Hex Barn Antiques
RD 1
Lenhartsville, Pa. 19534
(215)562–8433

Colonial Arms Antiques at
Highcroft
441 York Road
Route 202
New Hope, Pa. 18939
(215)862–2366

Country Antiques at
the Church
Route 202 and Upper
Mountain Road
RD 1/Box 58A
New Hope, Pa. 18938
(215)794–5009

Olde Hope Antiques
Box 69C/Route 202
New Hope, Pa. 18938
(215)794–8161

The Hanging Lamp Antiques
140 North State Street
Newtown,
Pa. 18940
(215)968–2015

The Village Smithy
149 North State Street
Newtown, Pa. 18940
(215)968–2149

Allen Antiques
Whitehall Road/RD 3
Norristown, Pa. 19401
(215)272–3341

Irons Antiques
RD 2/Box 417
Northampton, Pa. 18067
(215)262–9335

James and Nancy Glazer
2209 Delancey Place
Philadelphia, Pa. 19103
(215)732–8788

Mitchell and Susan Bunkin
RD 1/Box 423
Pipersville, Pa. 18947
(215)297–8653

Brandegee Antiques, Inc.
5639 Bartlett Street
Pittsburgh, Pa. 15217
(412)521–7583

Bower's Antiques
Route 212
Pleasant Valley, Pa. 18951
(215)346–8295

Russell E. Hill Antiques
1465 N.W. End Boulevard
Route 309
Quakertown, Pa. 18951
(215)536–8594

B and S Antiques
Corner Route 897 and
Mechanic Street
Reinholds, Pa. 17569
(215)267–2300

Audrey and Ed Kornowski
Box 115
Uwchland, Pa. 19480
(215)827–7654

*HARTMAN/CHRIS MEAD

265

Harry B. Hartman*
452 East Front Street
Marietta, Pa. 17547
(717)426–1474

de Vitry Primitives
285 West Main Street
Route 23
New Holland, Pa. 17557
(717)354–7910

Poole Antiques
RD 1/Route 202 and
Ingham Road
New Hope, Pa. 18939
(215)862–2919

Manford J. Robinson
4 Walton Drive
New Hope, Pa. 18939
(215)862–5914

Florence Schwartz
121 University Place
Oakland Pittsburgh, Pa. 12513
(412)521–1005
(412)621–2107

M. Finkel and Daughter
936 Pine Street
Philadelphia, Pa. 19107
(215)627–7797

Diana H. Bittel Antiques
1829 Old Gulph Road
Villanova, Pa. 19085
(215)527–0693

Marilyn J. Kowaleski
RD 3
Wernersville, Pa. 19565
(215)678–9948

C. L. Prickett, Inc.
Stony Hill Road
Yardley, Pa. 19067
(215)493–4284

Thanewold
P.O. Box 104
Zieglerville, Pa. 19492
(215)287–9258

RHODE ISLAND

The Farmer's Daughter
Route 2/South County Trail
Exeter, R.I. 02822
(401)295–8493

Hickory Hollow Antiques
Trimtown Road
North Scituate, R.I. 02857
(401)647–5321

Bayberry Acres Antiques
Matitty Road
North Smithfield, R.I. 02876

Edward and Joan Steckler
168 Governor Street
Providence, R.I. 02906
(401)272–1978

Dove and Distaff Antiques
472 Main Street
Wakefield, R.I. 02879
(401)783–5714

Stephanie A. Wood
Warwick, R.I.
(401)884–8272

Old Theatre Store
Route 102/Phillips Street
Wickford, R.I. 02852
(401)884–6020

SOUTH CAROLINA

Garden Gate Antiques
96 King Street
Charleston, S.C. 29401
(803)722–0308

TEXAS

Robert E. Kinnaman and
Brian Ramaekers
River Oaks Center at
2002 Peden Street
Houston, Texas 77019
(713)526–0095

VERMONT

The Sampler Shop
176 Washington Street
Barre, Vt. 05641
(802)479–2865

Belmont Antiques
Box 63
Belmont, Vt. 05730
(802)259–2338

Four Corners East Antiques
802 Main Street/Route 9
Bennington, Vt. 05201
(802)442–2612

Matteson Antiques
South Street/Grandview on
Route 7
Bennington, Vt. 05201
(802)442–9596
(802)442–6242

Betty Towne Antiques
520 South Street/Box 97
Bennington, Vt. 05201
(802)442–9204

The Brandon Antiques Center
Route 7
Brandon, Vt. 65733
(802)247–6721

Agnes and Bill Franks
55 Franklin Street/Route 7
Brandon, Vt. 05733
(802)247–3690

H. Cray Guildersleeve
57 Park Street
Brandon, Vt. 05733
(802)247–6684

Mrs. S. V. Holden
Routes 5 and 9
Brattleboro, Vt. 05301
(802)254–4725

The Chestnut Tree
Route 7
F. H. Horsford Nursery
Charlotte, Vt. 05445
(802)425–2811

New England Shoppe
Antiques
Route 7
Charlotte, Vt. 05445
(802)425–3219

Harold Smith
Antique Furniture
Route 30/Box 663
Dorset, Vt. 05251
(802)867–2271

Ice Pond Farm Antiques
Box 275
East Arlington, Vt. 05252
(802)375–6448

*GEAR DESIGN/RAYMOND WAITES

Farr's Antiques
Route 110/Washington Road
East Barre, Vt. 05649
(802)476–4308

Glenorton Country Antiques
Route 104
Fairfax, Vt. 05454
(802)849–3391

Gabriel's Barn
Woodchuck Hill Farm
Middletown Road
Grafton, Vt. 05146
(802)843–2398

Grafton Antiques
Route 121
Grafton, Vt. 05146
(802)843–2254

Woodshed Antiques
Grafton, Vt.
(802)843–2356

Thomas Hannan
American Antiques
Location:
Pockers Corner
Guilford, Vt.
Mail:
Box 159/RFD 3
Brattleboro, Vt. 05301
(802)254–2627

Barbara E. Mills Antiques
Route 5
Hartland, Vt. 05048
(802)436–2441

Dore B. McKennis
Route 30
Jamaica, Vt. 05343
(802)874–7191

Hearthstone Antiques
Route 11
Londonderry, Vt. 05148
(802)824–6893

Bix Antiques and Treasures
RD 3/Route 116
Middlebury, Vt. 05753
(802)388–2277

Peter Hawkes Limited
Frog Hollow Mill
Middlebury, Vt. 05753
(802)388–7424

The Village Store of
Middlebury
Route 7 South
Middlebury, Vt. 05753
(802)388–6476

First Republic Antiques
24 Liberty Street
Montpelier, Vt. 05602

Betty Sterling
Brainstorm Farm
Peth Road/Route 12 North
Randolph, Vt. 05060
(802)728-9114

Colonial House Antiques
Main Street/Box B
Randolph Center, Vt. 05061
(802)728-5571

John and Nancy Stahura
Mill Brook Antiques
Route 106
Reading, Vt. 05062
(802)484-5942

Weatherwell Antiques
Route 106
Reading, Vt. 05062
(802)484-7489

Schoolhouse Antiques
Route 121
Saxtons River, Vt. 05154
(802)869-2332

Sign of the Raven
Main Street
Saxtons River, Vt. 05154
(802)869-2500

Gadhue's Antiques
Route 7
Shelburne, Vt. 05482
(802)985-2682

Ethan Allen Antique
Shop, Inc.
1626 Williston Road
South Burlington, Vt. 65401
(802)863-3764

Fraser's Antiques
Route 143
Springfield, Vt. 05156
(802)885-4838

Green Mountain Antiques
of Stowe
Box 1003/Main Street
Stowe, Vt. 05672
(802)253-4369

William D. Benton Antiques
Vergennes, Vt.
(802)877-2815

Old Stone House
RFD 1
Vergennes, Vt. 05491
(802)759-2134

The House of Yesteryear
10 North Main Street
Wallingford, Vt. 05773
(802)446-2415

Yankee Maid Antiques
Route 7
Wallingford, Vt. 05773
(802)446-2463

Gay Meadow Farm
Antiques, Inc.
Trout Club Road
Weston, Vt. 05161
(802)824-6386

Hillary Underwood
21 Pleasant Street
Woodstock, Vt. 05091
(802)457-1750

Wood Shed Antiques
Route 12 North
Woodstock, Vt. 05091
(802)457-2490

VIRGINIA

Falquier and Harned Limited
The Atrium
277 South Washington Street
Alexandria, Va. 22314
(703)549-1750

Norma and William Wangel
34 East Loudoun Street
Leesburg, Va. 22075
(703)777-6991

Vicki Sandberg
9027 Traveller Street
Manassas, Va. 22110
(703)369-1101

*NEWCOMER/FRANK KOLLEOGY

Worcester House Antiques
U.S. 13
New Church, Va. 23415
(804)824-3847

Cochran's Antiques
P.O. Box 74
Purcellville, Va. 22132
(703)338-7395

Jeffrey and C. Jane Camp
American Folk Art Company
310 Duke Street
Tappahannock, Va. 22560
(804)443-2655

WASHINGTON, D.C.

Cherishables
1816 Jefferson Place N.W.
Washington, D.C. 20036
(202)785-4087

WEST VIRGINIA

Seeley Pine Furniture and
Antiques
Route 522 South
Berkley Springs, W. Va. 25411
(304)258-2343

Mary Longsworth Antiques
1141 Washington Street
Harpers Ferry, W. Va. 25425
(304)535-2385

John C. Newcomer *
1200 Washington Street
Harpers Ferry, W. Va. 25425
(304)535-6902

William Payne Antiques
Box 471
Harpers Ferry, W. Va. 25425
(304)535-2406

Morgan Lee Anderson
Americana
P.O. Box 647
Shepherdstown, W. Va. 25443
(304)897-6287

WISCONSIN

Furniture Doctors
25 South Main Street
Hartford, Wis. 53027
(414)673-3100

Jaeger Antiques
459 South Randall Avenue
Janesville, Wis. 53545
(608)754-8585

Mindy's Antiques
W220 N5651 Townline Road
Sussex, Wis. 53089
(414)246-3183

DIRECTORY OF CONTEMPORARY MANUFACTURERS AND SOURCES

The *Directory of Contemporary Manufacturers and Sources* lists articles being made today that can furnish and accessorize a country-style house. Many of these reproductions and adaptations are less expensive than their antique counterparts and are generally more readily available. In addition, many of these items are handcrafted and possess a special quality of their own, reflecting the current interest in arts and crafts. Next to the names in the following listing, there may be an (M) or a (T). The (M) denotes a large manufacturer, where most often direct purchasing is not possible, but one may call or write for a local distributor of the product. The (T) denotes that the merchandise is sold at that location "to the trade only," or, more specifically, to decorators. However, many of these articles are sold at retail outlets, so it is advised to write or call for shopping information.

ACCESSORIES

Ivan Barnett
RD 1
Stevens, Pa. 17578
(717)738–1590
Original handcrafted weather vanes. Custom work on request. Mail-order services available.

Barton's Baskets Etc.
P.O. Box 67
Forkland, Ala. 36740
(205)289–3611
Assorted split oak baskets. Mail-order services available.

The Bayberry
Montauk Highway
Amagansett, N.Y. 11930
(516)267–3000
Handmade traditional copper weather vanes. Mail-order services available.

Bay Country Woodcrafts
Route 13
Oak Hall, Va. 23416
(804)824–5626
Solid pine decorative waterfowl carvings, in kit form or finished. Mail-order services available.

Margie Caldwell
Box 1416
Sun Valley, Idaho 83353
(208)726–9270
Pine-needle baskets. Mail-order services available.

The Candle Cellar
and Emporium
1914 North Main Street
Fall River, Mass. 02720
(617)679–6057
(401)624–9529
Knife and candle boxes that fasten to wall, workmen's toolboxes. Mail-order services available.

Coker Creek Crafts
P.O. Box 95
Coker Creek, Tenn. 37314
(615)261–2157
Traditional and contemporary handmade white oak splint baskets. Mail-order services available.

The Decorator Emporium
Hardware, Inc.
353 Main Street
Danbury, Conn. 06810
(203)748–2648
Handmade weather vanes. Mail-order services available.

William Hale
P.O. Box 241 DTS
Portland, Maine 04112
(207)775–2165
Wooden rocking horses. Mail-order services available.

Bryant Holsenbeck
P.O. Box 162
Carrboro, N.C. 27514
Baskets of wild grape, reed, and wisteria. Custom work on request. Mail-order services available.

Ivy Products, Inc. (M)
Box 71
New Braintree, Mass. 01531
(617)867–8311
Assorted brooms, bellows.

Kari Lønning
36 Mulberry Street
Ridgefield, Conn. 06877
(203)431–0617
Contemporary baskets of dyed and natural rattan, often woven with seagrass.

Mainly Baskets
1771 Tully Circle, N.E.
Atlanta, Ga. 30329
(404)634–7664
(404)633–8690
Many baskets, including

reproduction American baskets, pinecone designs in heart-shaped form, wreaths.

MaLeck Industries, Inc. (M)
P.O. Box 247
Wingate, N.C. 28174
(704)233–4031
New Country Gear soap and bath accessories.

Charles Marchant Studios (M)
663 Fifth Avenue, 6th Floor
New York, N.Y. 10022
(212)595–9470
(212)757–6454
Decorative decoupage accessories in limited editions.

Kay Marshall
2201 Anton Way
Anchorage, Alaska 99503
(907)276–4932
Handmade denim dolls. Mail-order services available.

F. O. Merz and Company (M)
Brandywine Corporate Park
Wilson Drive
Westchester, Pa. 19380
(215)431–7500
Varied assortment of baskets.

Palecek Imports (M)
P.O. Box 2943
San Francisco, Calif. 94111
(415)398–1569
Varied assortment of baskets.

Joe Panzarella &
Jane Byrne Panzarella
High Point Crafts
RD 2/Sky High Road
Tully, N.Y. 13159
(315)696–8540
Woven fireplace brooms, feather dusters, bellows.

Peterboro Basket Co. (M)
Peterboro, N.H. 03458
(603)924–3861
Baskets, Early American buckets.

Primitive Artisan (M)
125 West Main Street
Plainville, Conn. 06062
(203)747–5704
Third-world baskets of many
varieties.

David Ritter
101 North Haggin
P.O. Box 2108
Red Lodge, Mont. 59068
(406)446–1227
Hand-carved ducks and
geese.

Ship 'N Out
934 Harmony Road
Pawling, N.Y. 12564
(914)878–4901
Nineteenth-century
reproduction copper
weather vanes. Mail-order
services available.

Jane Snead Samplers
Box 4909
Philadelphia, Pa. 19119
(215)848–1577
Old-fashioned sampler kits.
Mail-order services available.

Spaulding and Frost (M)
Main Street
Fremont, N.H. 03044
(603)895–3372
(603)895–4590
Finished and unfinished
wooden barrels, buckets,
baskets, boxes.

Sumac
P.O. Box 126
New Lebanon, N.Y. 12125
Baskets.

Veasey Studios
16 Gill Drive
Newark, Del. 19713
Decorative wildfowl carvings,
pewter, decoys.

West Rindge Baskets, Inc.
Box 24

Rindge, N.H. 03461
(603)899–2231
Handwoven New England
baskets.

Wildfowler Decoys (M)
56 Park Avenue
Babylon, N.Y. 11702
(516)587–7974
Hand-painted decorative
decoys, shorebirds.

Contemporary Primitive Paintings

Phyllis Aycock
1737 York Avenue, Apt. 5M
New York, N.Y. 10028
(212)860–5526
Custom primitive portraits,
original primitive paintings,
reproductions of antique
primitive portraits, still lifes,
landscapes, seascapes.

Pattie K. Bryant
Mailing Address:
P.O. Box 621
Southport, Conn. 06490
Studio Location:
30 Diving Street
Stonington, Conn. 06378
(203)535–3900
Contemporary primitive
painter specializing in
18th-century children, ships,
landscapes.

Betty W. McCool
P.O. Box 241
Heritage Hall
Ridgeland, Miss. 39157
(601)856–4082
Contemporary primitive
paintings, aged and cracked
to simulate aging of 200
years.

Random and Width
P.O. Box 427
West Chester, Pa. 19380
(215)436–4630
Reproduction folk art prints.

Barbara and Daniel Strawser
126 Main Street and
Stouchsburg
Womelsdorf, Pa. 19567
(215)589–4651
Folk paintings, wood
carvings.

Pat Thomas, Art Cellar
6708 Maple Terrace
Wauwatosa, Wis. 53213
(414)453–8971
Contemporary primitive
paintings.

Webb and Parsons
134 Elm Street
New Canaan, Conn. 06840
(203)966–1400
Contemporary folk paintings,
carvings.

EQUIPMENT

Appliances

Amana Refrigeration, Inc. (M)*
Amana, Iowa 52204
(319)622–5511

Kitchen appliances: freezers,
refrigerator/freezers, room
air conditioners, ranges,
dehumidifiers, microwave
ovens, cook tops, wall ovens,
trash compactors.

*AMANA/GEAR DESIGN/ROBERT GRANT

Braun Appliances U.S.A. (M)
55 Cambridge Parkway
Cambridge, Mass. 02142
(617)492–2100
Small kitchen appliances:
coffee grinders, coffee mills,
coffee makers, slicers, citrus
juicers, multipress juice
extractors, multipurpose
kitchen machines.

Caloric Corporation (M)*
Topton, Pa. 19562
(215)682–4211
Gas, electric, and
combination microwave
kitchen ranges.

*CALORIC/GEAR DESIGN/ROBERT GRANT

Garland Commercial Industries, Inc. (M)
Freeland, Pa. 18224
(717)636–1000
Commercial ranges.

The General Electric Company (M)
800 Third Avenue
New York, N.Y. 10022
(212)750–3461
Kitchen appliances.

KitchenAid (M)
Hobart Corporation
Troy, Ohio 45373
(513)335–7171
Kitchen appliances.

270

Maytag Company (M) *
403 West Fourth Street North
Newton, Iowa 50208
(515)792–7000
Kitchen appliances.

Vulcan-Hart Corporations (M)
3600 North Point Boulevard
Baltimore, Md. 21222
(301)284–0660
Commercial ranges.

Bathroom Fixtures

Baldwin/Tubs, Inc. *
At the head of Morgan Bay
Surry, Maine 04684
(207)667–8328
Handcrafted wooden tubs.

* BALDWIN/TUBS, INC.

Fife's Woodworking and Mfg.
Route 107
Northwood, N.H. 03261
(603)942–8339
Handcrafted solid wood bathroom accessories, including toilet seats and medicine cabinets. Custom woodworking on request. Mail-order services available.

Heads Up, Inc. (M)
14452 Franklin Avenue
Tustin, Calif. 92680
(714)544–0500
Oak bathroom furnishings, vanities, storage cabinets, pull-chain toilets, tank toilets, medicine cabinets, oak-trimmed mirrors.

Kohler Co. (M)
Kohler, Wis. 53044
(414)457–4441
Bathroom furnishings, including enameled cast-iron sinks and tubs.

The Tile Shop
1577 Solano Avenue
Berkeley, Calif. 94704
(415)525–4312
Stoneware sinks. Custom work on request. Mail-order services available.

Hardware

Baldwin Hardware Manufacturing Corp. (M)
841 Wyomissing Boulevard
Reading, Pa. 19603
(215)777–7811

Authentically reproduced brass hardware: locks, knobs, pulls; Limoges porcelain lever handles; hand-forged iron thumb latches.

Cassidy Bros. Forge
Route 1
Rowley, Mass. 01969
(617)948–7611
Wrought-iron fireplace tools and accessories, hardware, architectural ironwork. Mail-order services available.

The Decorator Emporium Hardware, Inc.
353 Main Street
Danbury, Conn. 06810
(203)748–2648
Authentically reproduced colonial hardware. Mail-order services available.

John Graney
Bear Creek Forge
Route 2/Box 135
Spring Green, Wis. 53588
(608)588–2032
Decorative and functional ironwork: andirons, colonial cooking hardware, kitchen racks, triangle dinner gongs. Custom work on request. Mail-order services available.

Hubbardton Forge and Wood S.R.
Boomoseen, Vt. 05732
(802)273–2047
Decorative and architectural wrought-iron products.

Steve Kayne Hand Forged Hardware
17 Harmon Place
Smithtown, N.Y. 11787
(516)724–3669
Fireplace tools and accessories; forged steel, brass, copper; military

accouterments; builder's hardware; hand-cast brass and bronze; household hardware; repairs, restorations. Mail-order services available.

Charles Lapen
Route 9/P.O. Box 529
W. Brookfield, Mass. 01585
(617)867–3997
Blacksmith and bronze molder. Mail-order services available.

Kenneth Lynch and Sons
78 Danbury Road
Wilton, Conn. 06897
(203)539–0532
Wrought-iron products.

Newton Millham Star Forge
672 Drift Road
Westport, Mass. 02790
(617)636–5437
Hand-forged hardware and 18th-century hearth cooking iron. Mail-order services available.

Old Guilford Forge
Mail Order:
1840 Boston Post Road
Retail:
76 Broad Street
Guilford, Conn. 06437
(203)453–2731
Hand-forged wrought-iron products, including fireplace equipment and hardware. Mail-order services available.

Virginia Metalcrafters, Inc. (M)
1010 East Main Street
Waynesboro, Va. 22980
(703)942–8205
Fireplace accessories, door knockers, footscrapers, doorstops.

Wallin Forge
Route 1/Box 65
Sparta, Ky. 41086
(606)567–7201

* MAYTAG CO./GEAR DESIGN/ ROBERT GRANT

Hand-forged ironware: utensil and pot racks, fireplace accessories, hardware. Custom work on request. Mail-order services available.

Table Linens

Laura Ashley, Inc.
714 Madison Avenue
New York, N.Y. 10021
(212)371–0606
Other shops located in San Francisco; Washington, D.C.; Boston; Chicago; Westport, Conn.; Ardmore, Pa.
Table linens of Laura Ashley fabrics. Mail-order services available.

Barth & Dreyfuss (M)*
2260 East 15th Street
Los Angeles, Calif. 90021
(213)627–6051
Kitchen accessories, including towels, aprons, mitts, pot holders, vinyl tablecloths; Christmas kitchen towels.

Geno Designs (M)
225 Fifth Avenue
New York, N.Y. 10010
(212)679–1877
Table linens in country prints.

Goodwin Weavers
Blowing Rock Crafts, Inc.
P.O. Box 314
Blowing Rock, N.C. 28605
(704)295–3577
Woven table linens. Mail-order services available.

Homespun Weavers
169 Ridge Street
Emmaus, Pa. 18049
(215)967–4550
Cotton homespun table linens, kitchen towels. Mail-order services available.

Leacock & Co., Inc. (M)*
1040 Avenue of the Americas
New York, N.Y. 10018
(212)398–9950
New Country Gear collection of table linens in country-style prints.

The Patchworks (M)
Division of Turkey Two
Box 183
Ellis Grove, Ill. 62241
(618)859–2640
Hand-sewn table linens.

Sel-Bar Weaving, Inc. (M)
P.O. Box 631
Newport, Vt. 05855
(802)334–6565
Woven table linens.

H. J. Stotter (M)
225 Fifth Avenue
New York, N.Y. 10010
(212)689–9800
Country-style table linens.

Marjorie S. Yoder
North Street/Box 181
Morgantown, Pa. 19543
(215)286–5490
Hand-stenciled table linens.

Tabletop and Kitchenware

Ball Corp. (M)
345 South High Street
Munsie, Ind. 47305
(317)747–6100
Glass jars for canning, preserving.

Beaumont Heritage Pottery
Beach Ridge Road/Box 293
York, Maine 03909
(207)363–5878
Handcrafted pottery.

Bennington Potters North (M)
324 County Street
Bennington, Vt. 05201
(802)863–2221
Bennington pottery.

Bowman's Pottery (M)
RFD 1
Fairfax, Vt. 05454
(802)849–6986
Varied assortment of pottery.

Breninger Taylor
Mansion Pottery
Taylor Mansion
476 South Church Street
Robesonia, Pa. 19551
(215)693–5344
Slipware, pottery, toys, sgraffito plates. Mail-order services available.

Linda & André Brousseau (M)
The Elements Pottery
629 North 3rd Street
Danville, Ky. 40422

(606)236–7467
Stoneware dinnerware. Mail-order services available.

Anne Burnham and
Gary Quirk Potters
Star Route/Picketville Road
Parishville, N.Y. 13672
(315)265–3175
Hand-built and thrown stoneware, porcelain.

Commercial Aluminum
Cookware Co. (M)
P.O. Box 583
Toledo, Ohio 43693
(419)666–8700
Heavy-duty aluminum cookware, also Calphalon black aluminum cookware with nonstick surface.

Copco, Inc. (M)
11 East 26th Street
New York, N.Y. 10010
(212)889–4500
Housewares and cookware, including "Country Clay" specialty baking dishes.

Corning Glass Works (M)
Corning, N.Y. 14830
(518)974–9000
Cookware.

Delaware Pottery
P.O. Box 105
Hope, N.J. 07840
(201)459–4023
Stoneware. Mail-order services available.

Denby Ltd., Inc. (M)
130 Campus Plaza
Edison, N.J. 08817
(201)225–4710
Country-style stoneware.

The Foltz Pottery
RD 1
Reinholds, Pa. 17569
(215)267–2676
Red clay pottery.

271

General Housewares
Corp. (M)
Cookware Group
P.O. Box 4066
Terre Haute, Ind. 47804
(812)234–3739
Blue-and-white enameled
cookware with plates and
cups; black cast-iron
cookware.

Gilmor Glassworks
Drawer H/Route 82
Pine Plains, N.Y. 12567
(518)398–6678
Functional and decorative
contemporary hand-blown
glass. Mail-order services
available.

Hartstone, Inc. (M)
P.O. Box 400
East Hanover, N.J. 07936
(201)884-0831
New Country Gear ceramic
dinnerware and cookware.

Jepcor International (M)
41 Madison Avenue
New York, N.Y. 10010
(212)889–9010
Dinnerware.

Jori Hand Cast Pewter
Bucks County Pewterers, Inc.
P.O. Box 157
Jamison, Pa. 18929
(215)345–8891
Hand-cast pewter
hollowware. Mail-order
services available.

Jugtown Pottery
Route 2
Seagrove, N.C. 27341
(919)464–3266
Handcrafted earthenware
and stoneware. Mail-order
services available.

Kerr Glass (M)
Main Street
Sand Spring, Okla. 74063

(918)245–1313
Glass jars for canning,
preserving.

Lauffer (M)
Belmont Drive
Somerset, N.J. 08873
(201)356–7676
Stainless-steel flatware,
stoneware dinnerware.

Livingston Pottery (M)
Box 74
Livingston, N.Y. 12541
(518)851–9064
Hand-thrown and carved
porcelain for the table.

Diane Love
851 Madison Avenue
New York, N.Y. 10021
(212)879–6997
Mikasa collection, custom-
made table accessories,
baskets, silk flowers.

Mad River Pottery
RFD Box 28
Bristol, Vt. 05443
(802)453–3778
Stoneware. Mail-order
services available.

Mikasa (M)
41 Madison Avenue
New York, N.Y. 10010
(212)481–1521
China, stoneware.

Mirro Aluminum
Company (M)
Manitowoc, Wis. 54220
(414)684–4421
SilverStone lined nonstick
heavy-duty brushed
aluminum cookware.

Oxford Pewter
RD 2/Box 225
Warwick, N.Y. 10990
(914)258–4836
Cast pewter, pewter
objects.

Patrick's Rolling Pins (M)
William Patrick
RD 1
Arlington, Vt. 05250
Assorted woodenware,
specializing in
rolling pins, plates.

Pewter Cupboard
1776 Easton Road
Doylestown, Pa. 18901
(215)345–1759
Hand-cast pewter. Mail-order
services available.

Pfaltzgraff (M)
140 East Market Street
York, Pa. 17405
(717)845–5626
Stoneware, china.

The Pilgrim Glass Corp. (M)
225 Fifth Avenue
New York, N.Y. 10010
(212)679–5577
Reproductions of Early
American colored glass in
ruby, blue, topaz,
tangerine; cranberry
glass reproductions.

The Pottery/Ron Taylor
10800 E. 24 Highway
Sugar Creek, Mo. 64054
(816)833–0617
Functional, decorative
pottery. Mail-order services
available.

The Potting Shed
20 Beharrell Street/
P.O.Box 1287
W. Concord, Mass. 01742
(617)369–2981
Handcrafted pottery,
including Dedham pottery
reproductions.
Mail-order services
available.

Primitive Artisan (M)
125 West Main Street
Plainville, Conn. 06062

(203)747–5704
Decorative earthenware
pottery from Thailand,
Mexico, Sri Lanka.

Revere Copper &
Brass, Inc. (M)
Clinton, Ill. 61727
(217)935–3111
Cookware in solid copper
bonded to stainless steel.

The Robinson-Ransbottom
Pottery Co. (M)
Roseville, Ohio 43777
(614)697–7355
Blue and brown hand-
decorated spatterware
pottery serving pieces,
accessories.

Rowantrees Pottery (M)
Blue Hill, Maine 04614
(207)374–5535
Wheel-thrown dinnerware
and accessory pieces.

Rowoco Company (M)
700 Waverly Avenue
Mamaroneck, N.Y. 10543
(914)698–4002
Kitchen houseware tools.

Rubel & Co. (M)
225 Fifth Avenue/Room 700
New York, N.Y. 10010
(212)683–4400
Glassware, hand-painted
tinware, pewter, brass.

Scituate Potters, Inc.
Route 6/Old Danielson Pike
North Scituate, R.I. 02857
(401)647–5383
Stoneware.

Jay Thomas Stauffer
707 W. Brubaker Valley Road
Lititz, Pa. 17543
(717)626–7067
Pewter tableware. Mail-order
services available.

The Store Ltd.
Village of Cross Keys
Baltimore, Md. 21210
(301)323–2350
Pewter flatware.

Sun-glo (M)
P.O. Box 348
Chappaqua, N.Y. 10514
(914)238–5111
Swedish-style woodenware,
shelving, storage, wine racks,
stemware glass holders.

Sweetheart Pottery
Norman and Lila Bacon
P.O. Box 144
Woodstock, N.Y. 12498
(914)679–2622
One-of-a-kind whimsical
paintings on white
earthenware and porcelain
plates, planters, boxes,
vases.

Taylor & Ng (M)
P.O. Box 200
400 Valley Drive
Brisbane, Calif. 94005
(415)467–2600
Assorted kitchenware,
including flatware, pan racks,
pans.

Tibor & Gail's General Store
P.O. Box 501
Salamanca, N.Y. 14779
(716)945–3212
Enamelware. Mail-order
services available.

Wedgwood (M)
41 Madison Avenue
New York, N.Y. 10010
(212)532–5950
China, stoneware.

Wheaton Village
Millville, N.J. 08332
(609)825–6800, ext. 504
Handcrafted glass, pottery,
tinware.

Walter White
5126 Woodlawn Avenue N.
Seattle, Wash. 98105
(206)632–7391
Asparagus-handled pewter
flatware.

*WILTON ARMETALE

Wilton Armetale (M)*
18th and Franklin Streets
Columbia, Pa. 17512
(717)684–9000
Contemporary metal
dinnerware,
hollowware, tabletop
utensils, flatware, cookware.

Woodbury Pewterers
Route 6
Woodbury, Conn. 06798
(203)263–2668
Handmade pewter
reproductions. Mail-order
services available.

The Yankee Peddler (M)
Burkart Bros., Inc.
Verplanck, N.Y. 10596
(914)737–7900
Hand-painted American
country tinware.

Wood Stoves

Comforter Stove Works (M)
Box 175
Lochmere, N.H. 03252
(603)528–1855
Woodburning stoves for
heating.

The Decorator Emporium
Hardware, Inc.
353 Main Street
Danbury, Conn. 06810

(203)748–2648
Woodburning stoves,
fireplace inserts.

The Earth Stove, Inc. (M)
10425 S.W.
Tualatin-Sherwood Road
Tualatin, Oreg. 97062
(503)638–3502
Woodburning stoves for
heating.

Energy Harvesters Corp. (M)
Route 12/Box 19
Fitzwilliam, N.H. 03347
(603)585–3300
Woodburning stoves for
heating.

*KRISTIA ASSOCIATES

Kristia Associates*
343 Forest Avenue
P.O. Box 1118
Portland, Maine 04104
(207)772–2821
Norwegian Jøtul
woodburning stoves for
heating.

Quaker Stove Co., Inc. (M)
200 West Fifth Street
Lansdale, Pa. 19446
(215)362–2019
Woodburning stoves for
heating.

Russo Wood Stove
Manufacturing Corp. (M)
87 Warren Street
Randolph, Mass. 02368
(617)767–2521
Woodburning stoves for
heating.

Sierra Marketing, Inc. (M)
Box 346
Harrisonburg, Va. 22801
(703)434–3800
Energy-saving for the
fireplace.

Vermont Castings, Inc. (M)
Prince Street
Randolph, Vt. 05060
(802)728–3111
Woodburning stoves.

Washington Stove Works (M)
P.O. Box 687
Everett, Wash. 98201
(206)252–2148
Potbelly stoves for heating
and cooking.

273

FURNITURE

R. W. Alexander
Yesterday's Yankee
Lakeville, Conn. 06039
(203)435–9539 or 435–2431
Handcrafted traditional
American furniture, including
cupboards, chests, hutch
table, weavers furniture;
candle boxes; restoration of
antique furniture. Custom
work available.

American Drew (M)
P.O. Box HP3,
One Plaza Center
High Point, N.C. 27261
(919)889–0333
Traditional and
contemporary bedroom,
dining-room upholstered and
occasional furniture.

274

Artists Gardens (M)
6290 Bird Road
Miami, Fla. 33155
(305)661-6481
Twig furniture and furniture kits, pendulum chairs, hammocks.

Bedlam Brass Beds (M)
19–21 Fairlawn Avenue
Fair Lawn, N.J. 07410
(201)796-7200
Brass beds. Custom designs on request. Parts, components for restoration of antique brass beds.

Bernhardt Furniture Co. (M)
P.O. Box 740
Lenoir, N.C. 28645
(704)758-9811
Traditional and contemporary bedroom, dining-room upholstered and occasional furniture.

Bittersweet
P.O. Box 5
Riverton, Vt. 05668
(802)485-8562
Handcrafted American primitive furniture: cupboards, grandfather clocks, tables. Custom work available.

Brass Bed Company of America (M)
2801 East 11th Street
Los Angeles, Calif. 90023
(213)269-9465
Brass furniture; custom brass pieces.

David Brian Press
Stonehaven/Route 312
Brewster, N.Y. 10509
(914)279-5017
Traditional American handcrafted furniture; restoration of antique pieces.

Corinne Burke *
1 Forest Glen Road
New Paltz, N.Y. 12561
(914)255-1078
Upholstered reproduction furniture.

Douglas Campbell Co.
31 Bridge Street
Newport, R.I. 02840
(401)846-4711
Handcrafted reproductions of antique furniture: lowboys, highboys, chests, desks, wing chairs, side and arm chairs, Windsors, butterfly tables, drop-leaf tables, side tables, pencil-post beds, Sheraton-turned beds, Queen Anne beds, Hired man's beds, Chippendale beds, Shell-carved demidome corner or flat cupboards.

Cassidy Bros. Forge
Route 1
Rowley, Mass. 01969
(617)948-7611
Wrought-iron furniture.

Christopher Design
3701 Turtle Creek Boulevard
Dallas, Tex. 75219
(214)521-8469
Twig furniture.

Cohasset Colonials (M)
Cohasset, Mass. 02025
(617)383-0110
Reproduction furniture kits, including Windsor chairs, dining tables, settle benches, chests, tables, four-poster canopy beds, trundle beds, blanket chests.

Craig Nutt Fine Wood Works
2014 5th Street
Northport, Ala. 35476
(205)752-6535
Traditional American furniture: handcrafted beds, tables, cupboards, blanket chests; custom work.

Door Store *
1 Park Avenue
New York, N.Y. 10016
(212)679-9700
Other locations in the New York City area.
"Country garden" chairs.

Ethan Allen (M)
Ethan Allen Drive
Danbury, Conn. 06810
(203)743-8000
Traditional American upholstered and occasional furniture.

Great North Woods
425 Fifth Avenue
New York, N.Y. 10016
(212)889-0983
Other shop locations in New York City.
Contemporary country-style furniture.

Guild of Shaker Crafts
401 W. Savidge
Spring Lake, Mich. 49456
(616)846-2870
Authentic Shaker replicas: dining-room silver tray, back-slat bench, community dining table (trestle), oval boxes, blanket chest, utility bench, cupboard, chairs, washstand, Shaker bed, hogscraper candlestick, brooms, Shaker pegs and knobs, pegboards, chair tapes.

Habersham Plantation (M)
P.O. Box 1209
Toccoa, Ga. 30577
(404)886-1476
American primitive furniture, including hutch tables, cupboards, pie safes, shelving, chests, sideboards, ladder-back chairs, sleigh beds, tavern beds, canopy beds, coffee tables, blanket chests.

Harden Furniture Co. (M)
Mill Pond Way
McConnellsville, N.Y. 13401
(315)245-1000
Traditional pieces in the "Sleepy Hollow Collection": dining-room furniture and bedroom sets; upholstered and occasional furniture.

The Hitchcock Chair Co. (M)
Riverton, Conn. 06065
(203)379–8531
Specializing in maple and
cherry traditional furniture,
many with hand stenciling.

Kittinger Company (M)
1893 Elmwood Avenue
Buffalo, N.Y. 14207
(716)876–1000
Traditional American
furniture, including the
Williamsburg and Newport
reproductions of dining
tables, side tables, coffee
tables, secretary desks,
breakfronts,
sideboards,
chests, beds, chairs,
benches, sofas.

Knob Creek (M)
P.O. Box 995
Morganton, N.C. 28655
(704)437–8212
Traditional furniture.

Peter Kramer
Historic District
Washington, Va. 22747
(703)675–3625
Summer Showroom
Route 6A
Brewster, Mass. 02631
(617)896–7576
Colonial-style furniture.

Raimundo Lemus
125 Christopher Street
New York, N.Y. 10014
(212)691–4035
Handcrafted Shaker-style
furniture;
custom work
available.

Tom McFadden
Star Route 6200
Philo, Calif. 95466
(707)895–3627
Custom handcrafted
American furniture.

D. R. Millbranth
Cabinetmaker
Center Road
Rural Route 2
Box 462
Hillsboro, N.H. 03244
(603)464–5244
Custom handcrafted
furniture: Chippendale,
primitive,
Shaker pieces.

Thos. Moser, Cabinet Makers
Cobbs Bridge Road
New Gloucester, Maine 04260
(207)926–4446
Custom handmade American
traditional furniture,
including chests, cupboards,
trestle tables, harvest tables,
chair-tables, trundle beds,
pencil-post beds, tall clocks.

Orleans Carpenters
Box 107 C/Rock Harbor Road
Orleans, Mass. 02653
(617)255–2646
Colonial and Shaker
furniture,
household items.

Pennsylvania House (M)
137 N. 11th Street
Lewisburg, Pa. 17837
(717)523–1285
Traditional American
living-room,
dining-room,
and bedroom furniture;
upholstered and occasional
pieces.

Pot Covers (M)
101 West 28th Street
New York, N.Y. 10001
(212)594–5075
Twig furniture.

The Rocker Shop *
of Marietta, Georgia
1421 White Circle, N.W.
P.O. Box 12
Marietta, Ga. 30061
(404)427–2618
Brumby rocker with matching
footstool and lapboard,
child's rocker, dining chairs,
porch swing.

* ROCKER SHOP

The Seraph (M)
Route 148
Brookfield, Mass. 01506
(617)867–9353
Custom upholstered
reproduction furniture.

Shaker Workshops, Inc.
Box 1028
Concord, Mass. 01742
Shaker furniture kits. Mail-
order services available.

Stanton Woodcraft
Airport Road/P.O. Box 516
Stanton, Ky. 40380
(606)663–4246
Appalachia handcrafted
furniture, including
ladder-back rockers, chests,
Shaker tables, cannonball
bed, pedestal tables, harvest
tables, Shaker stands.

Sugar Hill Furniture (M)
Plymwood Furniture Corp.
Lisbon, N.H. 03585
(603)838–6677

Colonial and contemporary
upholstered and occasional
furniture.

Marion Travis
P. O. Box 292
Statesville, N.C. 28677
(704)872–8194
Showroom:
East Main Street
Troutman, N.C.
Handcrafted American
furniture: ladder-back chairs,
tables, benches, rockers,
stools, swings.

Workbench
470 Park Avenue South
New York, N.Y. 10016
(212)753–1173
Other locations in New York,
New Jersey, Connecticut,
Pennsylvania.
Contemporary country-style
furniture, accessories.

LIGHTING

275

Abolite Lighting Co., Inc. (M)
305 North Center
West Lafayette, Ohio 43845
(614)545–6374
Farm and factory lighting.

Antiquity Handcrafted
Artifacts Incorporated
255 North Barron Street
Eaton, Ohio 45320
(513)456–3388
Early American-style lighting
fixtures: sconces, lanterns,
candlesticks, chandeliers,
candle molds, tinware. Mail-
order services available.

Authentic Designs
330 East 75th Street
New York, N.Y. 10021
(212)535–9590
Handcrafted re-creations and
adaptations of early American
chandeliers and sconces.
Mail-order services available.

Baldwin Hardware
Manufacturing Corp. (M)
841 Wyomissing Boulevard
Reading, Pa. 19603
(215)777–7811
Brass candlestick lamps with
black stipple parchment or
white textured Belgian linen
shades, brass sconces.

Black Rock (M)
P.O. Box 282
Derry, N.H. 03038
(603)434–4521
Early American imitation
pewter sconces and candle
holders.

Bowman's Pottery (M)
RFD 1
Fairfax, Vt. 05454
(802)849–6986
Stoneware, hurricane lamps,
candlesticks.

Cassidy Brothers Forge
Route 1
Rowley, Mass. 01969
(617)948–7611
Wrought-iron lighting. Mail-
order services available.

Colonial Tin Craft
7805 Railroad Avenue
Cincinnati, Ohio 45243
(513)561–3942
Handcrafted Early American
lighting: lanterns, chandeliers,
sconces, candelabra, lamps.
Mail-order
services available.

The Decorator Emporium
Hardware, Inc.
353 Main Street
Danbury, Conn. 06810
(203)748–2648
Authentically reproduced
colonial-style lighting:
lamps, sconces, lanterns,
chandeliers.

Found, Inc. (M)
Box 576
Hope Valley, R.I. 02832
(401)539–2335
Candlesticks and accent
pieces made from old wool-
spinning spools.

•HERITAGE LANTERNS

Heritage Lanterns *
70 A Main Street
Yarmouth, Maine 04096
(207)846–3911
Reproductions and
adaptations of early lighting:
lanterns, sconces, electric
way candles, chandeliers,
lamps. Mail-order services
available.

Hubbardton Forge and Wood
S.R.
Boomoseen, Vt. 05732
(802)273–2047
Handcrafted colonial-style
lighting: candlesticks,
sconces, chandeliers. Mail-
order services available.

Hurley Patentee Manor
RD 7/Box 98A
Kingston, N.Y. 12401
(914)331–5414
Handcrafted reproductions of
18th- and 19th-century lighting
fixtures: sconces, lamps,
chandeliers. Mail-order
services available.

Jori Hand Cast Pewter
Bucks County Pewterers, Inc.
P.O. Box 157
Jamison, Pa. 18929
(215)345–8891

Hand-cast traditional pewter
candlesticks and sconces.
Mail-order services available.

Knob Creek (M)
P.O. Box 995
Morganton, N.C. 28655
(704)437–8212
Traditionally styled lamps
and sconces.

Charles Lapen
Route 9/P.O. Box 529
W. Brookfield, Mass. 01585
(617)867–3997
Hand-forged colonial
reproduction chandeliers and
candle stands; custom work
on request. Mail-order
services available.

Mad River Pottery
RFD/Box 28
Bristol, Vt. 05443
(802)453–3778
Stoneware chandeliers. Mail-
order services available.

Marle Co.
170 Summer Street
Stamford, Conn. 06901
(203)348–2645
Reproductions of early
American lanterns; custom
work on request. Mail-order
services available.

Newton Millham Star Forge
672 Drift Road
Westport, Mass. 02790
(617)636–5437
18th-century lighting: grease
lamps, trammel candle
holders, rushlights, table and
floor candlestands. Mail-
order services available.

Gates Moore
River Road, Silvermine
Norwalk, Conn. 06850
(203)847–3231
Handcrafted early American

lighting fixtures: chandeliers,
sconces, lanterns. Mail-order
services available.

Newstamp Lighting Co.
227 Bay Road
North Easton, Mass. 02356
(617)238–7071
Reproductions of early
lighting fixtures: chandeliers,
sconces, candle holders. Mail-
order services available.

Patti Bros.
Village Green
Route 27
Sudbury, Mass. 01776
(617)443–9412
Early American lighting
fixtures: chandeliers,
sconces, lamps,
candlesticks,
lanterns; custom work
on request. Mail-order
services available.

Period Lighting Fixtures
1 Main Street
Chester, Conn. 06412
(203)526–3690
Handmade reproductions of
early American lanterns,
chandeliers, sconces.
Mail-order
services available.

Jay Thomas Stauffer
707 W. Brubaker Valley Road
Lititz, Pa. 17543
(717)626–7067
Reproductions of colonial
pewter candlesticks. Mail-
order services available.

The Tin Bin
20 Valley Road
Neffsville, Pa. 17601
(717)569–6210
Handcrafted 18th- and 19th-
century reproductions of
sconces, chandeliers, wall
and post lanterns. Mail-order
services available.

276

Tyndale (M)
41 Madison Avenue
New York, N.Y. 10010
(212)889–1770
Traditionally styled lamps.

Village Lantern
P.O. Box 8C
598 Union Street
North Marshfield,
Mass. 02059
Handmade colonial design
lighting fixtures:
chandeliers, lanterns,
sconces; custom work
on request. Mail-order
services available.

Virginia Metalcrafters, Inc. (M)
1010 East Main Street
Waynesboro, Va. 22980
(703)942–8205
Early American lighting
fixtures: candlesticks,
chandeliers, sconces.

Wilton Armetale (M)
18th and Franklin Streets
Columbia, Pa. 17512
(717)684–9000
Colonial-style metal
candlesticks, sconces, lamps.

Yankee Craft Products (M)
Box 244
West Simsbury, Conn. 06092
(203)658–6953
Antique wooden bobbin
candlesticks.

Candles

Linda and André Brousseau
The Elements Pottery (M)
629 North 3rd Street
Danville, Ky. 40422
(606)236–7467
Rolled beeswax candles.

The Candle Cellar
and Emporium
1914 North Main Street
Fall River, Mass. 02720

(617)679–6057
(401)624–9529
Bayberry tapers. Mail-order
services available.

Electric Candle Mfg. Co.
60 Chelmsford Street
Chelmsford, Mass. 01824
(617)256–9972
Beeswax candle covers,
electric candles and bulbs.
Mail-order services
available.

The Foltz Pottery
RD 1
Reinholds, Pa. 17569
(215)267–2676
(215)929–2597
Hand-dipped candles.

S. And C. Huber
Accoutrements
82 Plants Dam Road
East Lyme, Conn. 06333
(203)739–0772
Hand-dipped candles.

Lenox Candles, Inc. (M)
P.O. Box 2806
Oshkosh, Wis. 54903
(414)231–9620
Candles.

MATERIALS

Bed Linens and Quilts

Shanti Benoit
Magic Corner Quilts
42255 Little Lake Road
Mendocino, Calif. 95460
(707)937–0825
(707)937–4147
Quilts.

N. H. Blanket
Main Street
Harrisville, N.H. 03450
(603)827–3333
Wool blankets. Mail-order
services available.

Bloomcraft (M)
295 Fifth Avenue
New York, N.Y. 10016
(212)683–8900
Bedspreads, draperies,
pillows, shower curtains.

Carol Brown
Boxway
Putney, Vt. 05346
(802)387–5875
Irish wool and cotton
bedspreads, plain or
patterned; blankets.
Mail-order services
available.

Cannon Mills (M)
1271 Avenue of the Americas
New York, N.Y. 10020
(212)957–2500
Traditional and contemporary
bed and bath linens.

Cantitoe Corners
36 West 20th Street
New York, N.Y. 10011
(212)929–5977
(914)778–3165
Appliqué quilt kits. Mail-
order services available.

Diane Jackson Cole
9 Grove Street
Kennebunk, Maine 04043
(207)985–7387
Wool coverlet in traditional
blooming leaf overshot
pattern. Mail-order services
available.

Continental Quilt Shop
129 East 57th Street
New York, N.Y. 10022
(212)752–7631
Goosedown quilts with
channel stitching or Swiss-
style tufted stitching. Mail-
order services available.

Laura A. Copenhaver
"Rosemont"
P.O. Box 149
Marion, Va. 24354
(703)783–4663
Coverlets, quilts, canopies.

Country Curtains
Stockbridge, Mass. 01262
(413)298–5565
Bedspreads, dust ruffles,
canopies. Mail-order
services available.

Sandi Dobson
115 Beaumont Street
Brooklyn, N.Y. 11235
(212)934–6858
Quilts and quilt piece
pillows.

Dundee Mills, Inc. (M)
111 West 40th Street
New York, N.Y. 10018
(212)840–7200
Towels in floral patterns
based on antique
country styles.

Fieldcrest Mills, Inc. (M)
60 West 40th Street
New York, N.Y. 10018
(212)398–9500
Traditional and contemporary
bed and bath linens.

Ginger Snap Station
P.O. Box 81086
Atlanta, Ga. 30366
(404)455–4104
Quilt kits, quilters' fabrics
and materials. Mail-order
services available.

Goodwin Weavers
Blowing Rock Crafts, Inc.
P.O. Box 314
Blowing Rock, N.C. 28605
(704)295–3577
Woven coverlets, afghans,
canopies.
Mail-order services
available.

Gutcheon Patchworks
611 Broadway
New York, N.Y. 10012
(212)673–0990
Quilt kits, quilting fabrics
and supplies. Mail-order
services available.

Habersham Plantation (M)
P.O. Box 1209
Toccoa, Ga. 30577
(404)886–1476
Woven bedspreads.

Jakson (M)
225 Fifth Avenue
New York, N.Y. 10010
(212)532–9393
New Country Gear shower
curtains, bathroom
accessories.

Kay Marshall
2201 Anton Way
Anchorage, Alaska 99503
(907)276–4932
Handmade wool blankets.
Mail-order services available.

Martex (M)
WestPoint Pepperell, Inc.
1221 Avenue of the Americas
New York, N.Y. 10020
(212)354–9150
Bed and bath products,
including linens, towels, quilts.

Nettle Creek Industries (M)
Box 9/Peacock Road
Richmond, Ind. 47374
(317)962–1555
Custom and ready-made
draperies, curtains,
bedspreads, comforters,
pillows in provincial print
fabrics.

The Patchworks (M)
Division of Turkey Two
Box 183
Ellis Grove, Ill. 62241
(618)859–2640
Hand-sewn patchwork pillows.

Puckihuddle Products, Ltd.
Box AW 5
Oliverea, N.Y. 12462
(914)254–5553
Handmade quilts, lacy and
appliquéd pillows. Mail-order
services available.

Quilts and Other Comforts
Box 394/
6700 West 44th Avenue
Wheat Ridge, Colo. 80033
Quilt kits. Mail-order
services available.

Tim and Maureen Rastetter
Rastetter Woolen Mill
Star Route
Millersburg, Ohio 44654
(216)674–2103
Handmade wool comforters,
goose-down comforters,
feather bedding. Mail-order
services available.

Riverdale Pillow
295 Fifth Avenue
New York, N.Y. 10016
(212)679-3636
New Country Gear decorative
pillows.

*SPRINGS MILLS, INC./GEAR DESIGN/RAYMOND WAITES

Springs Mills, Inc. (M)*
104 West 40th Street
New York, N.Y. 10018
(212)556-6186
Bed and bath linens,
including the
"Country Furrows"
Collection by Gear Design.

The Stearns and Foster Co. (M)
Creative Quilting Center
P.O. Box 15380
Cincinnati, Ohio 45215
(513)948–5295
Quilting patterns and
supplies. Mail-order services
available.

Sunshine Lane
Box 262 East
Millersburg, Ohio 44654
Quilts in original Amish
designs. Mail-order services
available.

Wamsutta (M)
111 West 40th Street
New York, N.Y. 10018
(212)930–5000
Traditional and contemporary
bed and bath linens.

Marjorie S. Yoder
North Street
Box 181
Morgantown, Pa. 19543
(215)286–5490
Hand-stenciled bed linens.

Curtains

Colonial Maid Curtains
Depot Plaza
Mamaroneck, N.Y. 10543
(914)698–6136
Authentic reproductions of
Early American-style

curtains. Mail-order services
available.

Constance Carol
Box 899
Plymouth, Mass. 02360
(617)746–6116
Other shop locations in
Plymouth, Mass.; Lexington,
Mass.; Williamsburg, Va.;
Philadelphia.
Early American and
contemporary custom and
ready-made curtains in
fabrics from Waverly,
Schumacher, Springs Mills,
Roclon Mills, Burlington.
Mail-order services available.

Laura A. Copenhaver
"Rosemont"
P.O. Box 149
Marion, Va. 24354
(703)783–4663
Ready-made curtains.

Country Curtains
Stockbridge, Mass. 01262
(413)298–5565
Ready-made Early American-
style curtains in cotton
muslin or permanent press.
Mail-order services available.

Croscill Curtain Co., Inc. (M)
261 Fifth Avenue
New York, N.Y. 10016
(212)689–7222
Ready-made curtains.

Fabrics and Wall Coverings

Laura Ashley, Inc.
714 Madison Avenue
New York, N.Y. 10021
(212)371–0606
Other shops located in
San Francisco; Washington,
D.C.; Boston; Chicago;
Westport, Conn.; Ardmore, Pa.
Coordinating fabrics and
wall coverings in country
prints. Mail-order services
available.

278

Birge Wallcoverings (M)
P.O. Box 27
Buffalo, N.Y. 14240
(716)891–8334
''Colonial and Country
Collections'' of wall
coverings based on
documentary patterns.

Bloomcraft (M)
295 Fifth Avenue
New York, N.Y. 10016
(212)683–8900
Traditional and contemporary
fabrics.

Carol Brown
Boxway
Putney, Vt. 05346
(802)387–5875
Irish tweeds and other
natural fiber fabrics for
upholstery and clothing,
curtain materials. Mail-order
services available.

Brunschwig and Fils (T)
979 Third Avenue
New York, N.Y. 10022
(212)838–7878
Other showroom locations in
Atlanta, Boston, Chicago,
Dallas, Los Angeles.
Traditional fabrics and
wall coverings.

China Seas (T)
149 East 72nd Street
New York, N.Y. 10021
(212)879–3100
Other showroom locations in
Atlanta, Boston, Chicago,
Dallas, Denver, Honolulu,
Houston, Los Angeles,
Philadelphia, Phoenix, San
Francisco, Seattle, Troy, Mich.
Fabrics and wall coverings
reflecting traditional
Chinese design motifs,
similar to Chinese export
fabrics and wall coverings of
the early
colonial period.

Clarence House (T)
40 East 57th Street
New York, N.Y. 10022
(212)752–2890
Other showroom locations in
Atlanta, Boston, Chicago,
Dallas, Houston, Los
Angeles, Miami,
Philadelphia, Portland, San
Francisco, Seattle. Traditional
fabrics, wall coverings,
trimmings.

Cohama/Riverdale (M)
200 Madison Avenue
New York, N.Y. 10016
(212)564–6000
New Country Gear collection
of prints and woven
fabrics.

Craft House
South England Street
Williamsburg, Va. 23185
(800)446–9240
Williamsburg documentary
fabrics.

Fabrications
146 East 56th Street
New York, N.Y. 10022
(212)371–3370
Other shops in the Boston
area.
Traditional American calicos,
muslin, chintz prints, novelty
woven fabrics of cotton and
linen. Mail-order services
available.

The Golden Ram
P.O. Box 246
Corner of Park and Evans
Christiansburg, Va. 24073
(703)382–0049
Colonial overshot
handwoven material. Mail-
order services available.

Gurian's
276 Fifth Avenue
New York, N.Y. 10001
(212)689–9696

Hand-embroidered crewel
fabric. Mail-order services
available.

S. M. Hexter Company (T)
2800 Superior Avenue
Cleveland, Ohio 44114
(216)696–0146
Showroom locations in
Atlanta, Boston, Dallas, Los
Angeles, New York.
Traditional and contemporary
fabrics and wall coverings.

Hinson and Company (T)
General Offices:
251 Park Avenue South
New York, N.Y. 10010
Showroom:
979 Third Avenue
New York, N.Y. 10022
(212)475–4100
Coordinated fabrics and wall
coverings.

Imaginations
61 Kendall Street
Framingham, Mass. 01701
(617)620–1411
Laura Ashley, Bloomcraft,
Covington, Cyrus Clarke,
Greeff, P. Kaufmann,
Cohama/Riverdale,
Schumacher, Waverly fabric
lines. Mail-order services
available.

*Imperial Wallcoverings *
Div. of Imperial Paper Co.
23645 Mercantile Road
Beachwood, Ohio 44122
(216)464–3700

Wall coverings in country
prints and natural colors.

Marimekko
7 West 56th Street
New York, N.Y. 10019
(212)581–9616
Fabrics and wall coverings in
contemporary country designs.

Nettle Creek (M)
Box 9/Peacock Road
Richmond, Ind. 47374
(317)962–1555
Provincial print fabrics.

Old Stone Mill Corp.
Route 8
Adams, Mass. 01220
(413)743–1015
(800)628–5046
Other showroom locations in
Atlanta, Boston, Chicago,
New York, Los Angeles.
Traditional and documentary
wall coverings and fabrics.
Mail-order services available.

La Provence de Pierre Deux
353 Bleecker Street
New York, N.Y. 10014
(212)675–4054
Other shop locations in
Atlanta, Bal Harbour, Beverly
Hills, Boston, Carmel, Chevy
Chase, Chicago, Kansas City,
Palm Beach, San Francisco,
Seattle.
Country French fabrics.

Raintree Designs (T)
979 Third Avenue
New York, N.Y. 10022
(212)477–8594
Other showroom locations in
Atlanta, Boston, Chicago,
Dallas, Detroit, Houston, Los
Angeles, Miami, New York,
Philadelphia, San Francisco,
Washington, D.C.
Laura Ashley country print
fabrics and
wall coverings.

279

Scalamandre (T)
950 Third Avenue
New York, N.Y. 10022
(212)361–8500
Other showroom locations in
Atlanta, Boston, Chicago,
Dallas, Houston, Los
Angeles, Philadelphia, San
Francisco.
Traditional fabrics, wall
coverings, trimmings.

F. Schumacher and Co. (T)
939 Third Avenue
New York, N.Y. 10022
(212)644–5900
Traditional and contemporary
fabrics and wall coverings.

Stroheim & Romann (T)
155 East 56th Street
New York, N.Y. 10022
(212)691–0700
Other showroom locations in
Atlanta, Boston, Chicago,
Dallas, Los Angeles,
Philadelphia, San Francisco.
Traditional fabrics.

Waverly Fabrics (T)
939 Third Avenue
New York, N.Y. 10022
(212)644–5900
Traditional and contemporary
fabrics and wall coverings.

Paint

Cohasset Colonials (M)
Cohasset, Mass. 02025
(617)383–0110
Oil-based paints in tradition
of Early American milk paint
colors. Mail-order services
available.

Finnaren and Haley, Inc. (M)
2320 Haverford Road
Ardmore, Pa. 19003
(215)649–5000
Interior and exterior paints
in authenticated shades used
during revolutionary period.

Fletcher's
Elm Street/Route 101 West
Milford, N.H. 03055
(603)673–2300
Other shop locations in N.H.
Interior paint in authentic
colonial colors. Mail-order
services available.

The Old Fashioned Milk
Paint Company (M)
Box 222
Groton, Mass. 01450
(617)448–6336
Milk paint in country colors.
Mail-order
services available.

*SHERWIN WILLIAMS/ROBERT GRANT

Sherwin Williams (M) *
101 Prospect Avenue
Cleveland, Ohio 44115
(216)566–2000
Paint in natural country
colors; available at 1,400
Sherwin-Williams stores
nationwide.

Turco Coatings, Inc. (M)
Wheatland and Mellon Streets
Phoenixville, Pa. 19460
(215)933–7758
Buttermilk paints. Mail-order
services available.

Rugs and Floor Treatments

Adams and Swett
380 Dorchester Avenue
Boston, Mass. 02127
(617)268–8000
Traditionally styled hand-
braided wool rugs. Mail-
order services
available.

Braid-Aid
466 Washington Street
Pembroke, Mass. 02359
(617)826–6091
Materials and accessories for
rug braiding and hooking,
quilting, shirret, weaving.
Mail-order services available.

Diane Jackson Cole
9 Grove Street
Kennebunk, Maine 04043
(207)985–7387
Handwoven wool strip rugs
with Irish linen warp and
braided ends. Mail-order
services available.

The Collector's Choice
404 East 14th Street
Apt. 5
New York, N.Y. 10009
(212)254–7744
Wool braided rugs in
traditional and
contemporary
designs.

Colonial Mills, Inc.
560 Mineral Spring Avenue
Pawtucket, R.I. 02860
(401)724–6279
Braided rugs. Mail-order
services available.

Laura A. Copenhaver
"Rosemont"
P.O. Box 145
Marion, Va. 24354
(703)783–4663
Hooked rugs.

Country Braid House
Clark Road
Tilton, N.H. 03276
(603)286–4511
Custom braided rugs, rug kits.

Craftswomen
Box 715
Doylestown, Pa. 18901
(215)822–0721
Custom-made canvas
floorcloths based on early
cloth and quilt patterns. Mail-
order services available.

Betty Emerson
108 New Haven Road
Oak Ridge, Tenn. 37830
(615)482–2943
Woven rugs and mats.

Floorcloths Incorporated
P.O. Box 812
Severna Park, Md. 21146
(301)647–3328
Custom-made canvas
floorcloths in documented
patterns. Mail-order services
available.

Kenneth Fortney
10 East Hazel Avenue
Marietta, Pa. 17547
(717)426–3151
Custom canvas floorcloths.

Habersham Plantation (M)
P.O. Box 1209
Toccoa, Ga. 30577
(404)886–1476
Rag rugs, braided rugs,
oriental carpets.

Heirloom Rugs
28 Harlem Street
Rumford, R.I. 02916
(401)438–5672
Hooked rug patterns. Mail-
order services available.

Heritage Rugs
Lahaska, Pa. 18931
(215)794–7229

Custom-made Early American rag rugs. Mail-order services available.

Alice Pickett, Handweaver *
194 Chestnut Street
Rehoboth, Mass. 02769
(617)252-3541
Custom-designed handwoven rugs. Mail-order services available.

Puckihuddle Products, Ltd.
Box A W 5
Oliverea, N.Y. 12462
(914)254-5553
Amish hand-loomed rugs. Mail-order services available.

Tim and Maureen Rastetter
Rastetter Woolen Mill
Star Route
Millersburg, Ohio 44654
(216)674-2103
Handmade rag rugs and rag carpeting. Mail-order services available.

Rosecore Carpet Co., Inc. (T)
979 Third Avenue
New York, N.Y. 10022
(212)421-7272
Other showrooms in Boston, Chicago, Dallas, Los Angeles, Philadelphia, San Francisco. Varied assortment of carpets, including rag rugs.

Stark Carpet Corp. (T)
979 Third Avenue
New York, N.Y. 10022
(212)752-9000
Other showrooms in Boston, Chicago, Dallas, Los Angeles. Varied assortment of carpets, including rag rugs.

Ernest Treganowan, Inc. (T)
306 East 61st Street
New York, N.Y. 10021
(212)755-1050
Custom braided and hooked rugs in traditional designs.

& Vice Versa (T)
979 Third Avenue
New York, N.Y. 10022
(212)477-9877
Other showrooms in Atlanta, Boston, Chicago, Dallas, Los Angeles.
Rag rugs by the yard.

Stenciling

Adele Bishop, Inc.
P.O. Box 122
Dorset, Vt. 05251
(802)867-2235
Stencil kits and supplies for boxes, tinware, furniture, walls, fabrics, floors, floorcloths. Mail-order services available.

The Clayton Store
RFD
Canaan, Conn. 06018
(413)229-2621
Restoration of stenciled, grained, and decorated surfaces on painted interiors and furniture; repairs of country furniture and accessories.

Kenneth Fortney
10 East Hazel Avenue
Marietta, Pa. 17547
(717)426-3151
Wall and floor stenciling in 18th- and 19th-century patterns and Victorian styles.

Pamela Friend
Hand Stenciled Interiors
590 King Street
Hanover, Mass. 02339
(617)878-7596
Custom stenciling, wall stencil kits.

Megan Parry
1727 Spruce
Boulder, Colo. 80302
(303)444-2724
Custom wall stenciling, mural services; restorations.

Stencil Magic
8 West 19th Street
New York, N.Y. 10011
(212)675-8892
Stencil kits. Mail-order services available.

Stenciled Interiors
Hinman Lane
Southbury, Conn. 06488
(203)264-8000
Custom floor and wall stenciling, stencil kits; restorations; lectures and workshops.

Virginia Teichner
Handcrafted Walls
P.O. Box 368
New Canaan, Conn. 06840
(203)355-1517
Custom wall and floor stenciling, primitive murals.

D. B. Wiggins
Hale Road
Tilton, N.H. 03276
(603)286-3046
Custom painting and stenciling of period interiors.

STRUCTURAL ELEMENTS

Flooring, Fans

American Olean Tile Co. (M)
Division of National Gypsum
1000 Cannon Avenue
Lansdale, Pa. 19446
(215)855-1111
Ceramic flooring, wall tiles.

American Woodcarving
282 San Jose Avenue
San Jose, Calif. 95125
(408)294-2968
Custom carved and raised panel doors.

The Broad-Axe Beam
RD 2/Box 181 E
West Brattleboro, Vt. 05301
(802)257-0064
Structural and decorative hand-hewn white pine beams.

Cape Cod Cupola
Company (M)
78 State Road/Route 6
North Dartmouth, Mass. 02747
(617)994-2119
Cupolas.

Country Floors
300 East 61st Street
New York, N.Y. 10021
(212)758-7414
Imported wall and floor tiles; handcrafted accessories such as planters, baskets, vases.

Dale Carlisle
Route 123
Stoddard, N.H. 03464
(603)446-3937
Wide pine boards and planks, pine clapboards, natural weathered boards and beams, cedar shingles.

Diamond K. Co., Inc. (M)
130 Buckland Road
South Windsor, Conn. 06074
(802)348-6347
Rustic weathered barn wood, hand-hewn beams, rough-cut weathered beams, wide plank pine and old wood clapboards.

Formica Corporation (M)
Subsidiary of American
Cyanamid Co.
Wayne, N.J. 07470
(201)831–1234
Formica panels and surface
coverings in country colors.

*GOULD INC./GEAR DESIGN/ROBERT GRANT

Gould Incorporated (M) *
811 North Main Street
Belfontaine, Ohio 43311
(513)593–6010
Fusable equipment, including
electro-strip lighting.

Guyon Industries, Inc. (M)
65 Oak Street
Lititz, Pa. 17543
(717)626–0225
Rustic wood products:
barn siding, pine clapboard
siding, rustic fencing, hewn
beams and timbers, wide
plank pine flooring, primitive
furniture; settler's cabins.

The House Carpenters
Box 217
Shutesbury, Mass. 01072
(413)256–8873
(413)253–7020
Traditional timber
frames of Massachusetts red
oak and white pine, with
joinery done in 18th-century
fashion; also old growth
southern yellow pine flooring.

Hunter Division (M)
Robbins and Myers
Incorporated
P.O. Box 14775
Memphis, Tenn. 38114
(901)743–1360
Ceiling fans.

Maurer & Shepherd, Joyners
122 Naubuc Avenue
Glastonbury, Conn. 06033
(203)633–2383
Colonial-style small pane
windows, sashes and frames,
wide pine flooring; custom
work available.

Preservation Resource Center
Lake Shore Road
Essex, N.Y. 12936
(518)963–7305
Window sashes.

SUPPLIERS

Chair Caning

The Anderson-Williams House
H. Joseph Williams
47 Mohican Road
Cornfield Point
Old Saybrook, Conn. 06475
(203)388–2587
Seat weaving in natural
rush, splint weaving, Shaker
tape; caning; wicker repair;
custom-made footstools and
doll chairs.

The Cane-ery
P.O. Box Drawer 17113
Nashville, Tenn. 37217
(615)776–2040
Chair-caning supplies.
Mail-order services available.

The Newell Workshop
19 Blaine Avenue
Hinsdale, Ill. 60521
(312)323–7367
Chair-caning kits and other
seat-weaving supplies.
Mail-order
services available.

Special Stores

Added Oomph! (T)
270 South Wrenn Street
High Point, N.C. 27260
(919)886–4410

Old and new items. Quilts,
twig furniture, tinware,
architectural items.

The Ark Gallery
Promise Hill Farm
Route 1
Maple Plain, Minn. 55359
(612)479–2575
Toys, fine arts, antiques with
an animal theme, including
wood carvings by Thomas
Langen, oil paintings by
Philo Levi (Chief) Willey and
Mattie Lou O'Kelley, graphics
by Kathy Jakobsen.

Around the Point Craft Coop
A Crafts Co-operative
Friendship Street
Waldoboro, Maine 04572
(207)832–4032
Handmade articles: pottery,
weaving, quilting, jewelry,
batik, hand-painted
and hand-forged items.

Bailey/Heubner at
Henri Bendel, Inc.
10 West 57th Street
New York, N.Y. 10019
(212)247–1100, ext. 339
Well-designed functional
articles for the home,
including summer furniture,
dinnerware, flatware,
kitchenware, baskets.

L. L. Bean, Inc.
Freeport, Maine 04033
(207)865–3111
Woodburning stoves, decoys,
blankets, fireside chairs, rope
hammocks, down comforter
kits, picnic baskets,
functional cookware, wooden
towel racks and dish racks
kerosene lamps, flannel
sheets. Mail-order services
available.

Berea College
Student Craft Industries
Berea, Ky. 40403
(606)986–9341
Handcrafted items, including
American furniture
reproductions: canopy frame
bed, spool bed, hired man's
bed, ladder-back side and
arm chairs; pottery; homespun
place mats and tablecloths;
dolls; brooms. Mail-order
services available.

Conran's
160 East 54th Street
New York, N.Y. 10022
(212)371–2225
Contemporary country
furniture, bed and bath
linens, fabrics, wall
coverings, floor coverings,
bathroom furnishings,
kitchenware, dinnerware,
lighting fixtures. Mail-order
services available.

Cumberland General Store
Route 3
Crossville, Tenn. 38555
(615)484–8481
Kerosene lamps, sconces,
cast-iron cookware, ceiling
fans, orchard and gardening
equipment, copperware,
stoneware, weather vanes,
wood stoves. Mail-order
services available.

Dean and De Luca, Inc.
121 Prince Street
New York, N.Y. 10012
(212)254–7774
46 Newtown Lane
East Hampton, N.Y. 11937
Assorted housewares,
accessories.

The Edison Institute
20900 Oakwood Boulevard
Dearborn, Mich. 48121
(313)271–1620, ext. 307
Reproductions from

Greenfield Village and Henry Ford Museum, including furniture from The Bartley Collection, Ltd.; clocks by Colonial of Zeeland; lamps by Norman Perry, Inc.; china by Hall China Co.; glassware by Fostoria Glass Co.; pewter by Woodbury Pewterers; fabrics and wallpaper by S. M. Hexter Co. Mail-order services available.

The Elder Craftsman
850 Lexington Avenue
New York, N.Y. 10021
(212)535–8030
Custom-made crafts, including theorems, afghans, appliquéd pillows, dried wreaths, needlepoint, crewel, crib quilts.

The Elements
Gallery for Contemporary American Crafts
766 Madison Avenue
New York, N.Y. 10021
(212)744–0890
14 Liberty Way
Greenwich, Conn. 06830
(203)661–0014
Handmade contemporary American crafts: ceramics, glass, wood, jewelry, fiber hangings, baskets, metalwork, selected clothing.

Pie Galinat
New York, N.Y.
(212)741–3259
Antique quilt restoration; custom-made stretchers for quilts and hooked rugs, rag carpets sewn together for area rugs.

The Gazebo
660 Madison Avenue
New York, N.Y. 10021
(212)832–7077
Handcrafted articles: quilts, handwoven rag rugs, wicker furniture, pillows.

*DAVIS MATHER/CHRIS MEAD

S. And C. Huber Accoutrements
82 Plants Dam Road
East Lyme, Conn. 06333
(203)739–0772
Textile and weaving tools and materials, handspun yarns, natural dyes, potpourri, candles, stoneware, lighting devices, soaps, stencils, woodenware. Mail-order services available.

The Mercer Museum Shop
The Bucks County Historical Society
Pine Street
Doylestown, Pa. 18901
(215)345–0210
Handcrafted items, including boxes, baskets, writing fixtures, redware, spongeware, toleware.

Museum Shop
Museum of American Folk Art
49 West 53rd Street
New York, N.Y. 10019
(212)581–2474
Books and objects relating to traditional American folk art. Mail-order services available.

Museum Shop
Museum of Fine Arts
29 Sleeper Street
Boston, Mass. 02210
(617)426–3123
Reproduction of a 19th-century lanterns, Shaker oval boxes, Peacock weather vane, footscraper, and needlepoint designs. Mail-order services available.

The New Englander, Inc.
5144 York Road
Holicong, Pa. 18928
(215)794–5663
Contemporary and antique items: lighting fixtures, furniture, accessory pieces.

Ozark Mountain Collection
7 Downing Street
P.O. Box 507
Hollister, Mo. 65672
(417)334–5788
Handcrafted one-of-a-kind pieces: wooden boxes, patchwork quilts, furniture.

Putumayo
857 Lexington Avenue
New York, N.Y. 10021
(212)734–3111

Contemporary and antique folk art, furniture, textiles, crafts.

The Renovator's Supply
71 Northfield Road
Millers Falls, Mass. 01349
(413)659–3542
Reproduction hardware, lighting, plumbing, building supplies, tools, accessories. Mail-order services available.

The Silo
Hunt Hill Farm
Upland Road
RFD 3
New Milford, Conn. 06776
(203)355–0300
Country kitchen arts and crafts items, including baskets, pottery, sculpture, weaving, hand-blown glass, stained glass. Mail-order services available.

Southern Highland Handicraft Guild
P.O. Box 9545
15 Reddick Road
Asheville, N.C. 28805
(704)298–7928
Handcrafted items, including furniture, straw brooms, baskets, weaving, pottery, metalwork, leatherwork; pinecone wreaths.

283

INDEX

Note: Page numbers in boldface indicate principal references to a subject.

287

Sword, Civil War, 57

T

V

W

Y

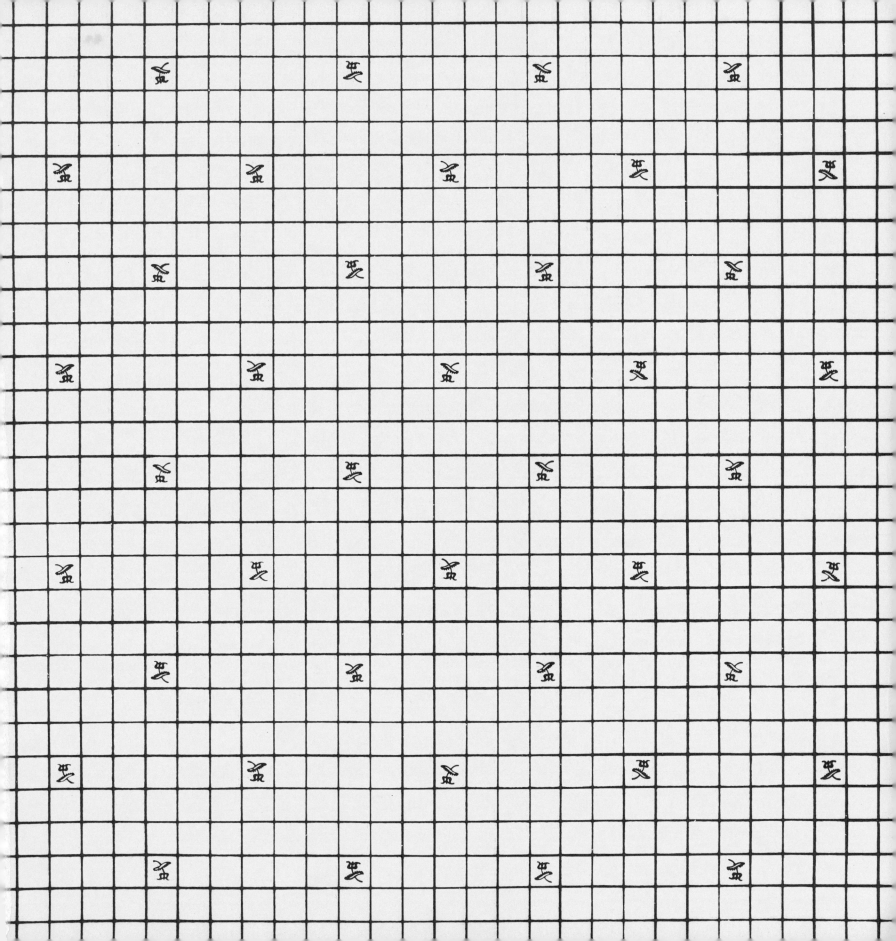

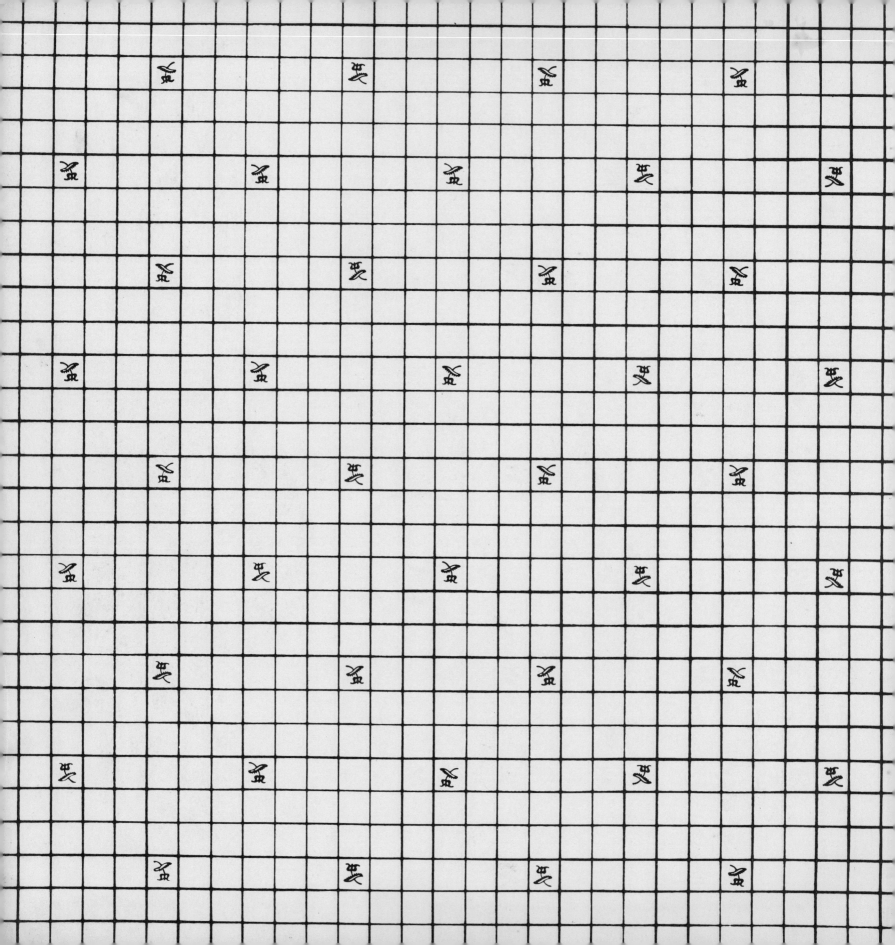